TELEVISION AND
LAW ENFORCEMENT

TELEVISION AND LAW ENFORCEMENT

By

JOSEPH MISSONELLIE, M.A.

Detective
Wyckoff Police Department
Wyckoff, New Jersey

and

JAMES S. D'ANGELO, M.A.

Supervisor/Teacher
Hawthorne Public School System
Hawthorne, New Jersey

CHARLES C THOMAS • PUBLISHER
Springfield • Illinois • U.S.A.

Published and Distributed Throughout the World by
CHARLES C THOMAS • PUBLISHER
2600 South First Street
Springfield, Illinois 62717

This book is protected by copyright. No part of it
may be reproduced in any manner without written
permission from the publisher.

© 1984 by CHARLES C THOMAS • PUBLISHER
ISBN 0-398-05007-4
Library of Congress Catalog Card Number: 84-211

With THOMAS BOOKS *careful attention is given to all details of manufacturing and design. It is the Publisher's desire to present books that are satisfactory as to their physical qualities and artistic possibilities and appropriate for their particular use.* THOMAS BOOKS *will be true to those laws of quality that assure a good name and good will.*

Printed in the United States of America
SC-R-3

Library of Congress Cataloging in Publication Data

Missonellie, Joseph.
  Television and law enforcement.

  Bibliography: p.
  Includes index.
  1. Television in police work—United States.   2. Law
enforcement—United States.   I. D'Angelo, James S.
II. Title.
HV7936.T4M57   1984   363.2'028   84-211
ISBN 0-398-05007-4

PREFACE

Recent advances in technology have provided law enforcement agencies with new tools to help improve their departmental operations. One such tool is television. Having proven itself in the commercial and entertainment arena, television is now taking its place in business, industry, education, and government.

Although it possesses tremendous potential in the law enforcement field, television has, until recently, been neglected. This has been due in part to excessive equipment costs. When video technology was first introduced to nonbroadcast, noncommercial users, its costs were astronomical, but today, equipment costs have decreased dramatically while overall quality and performance have increased significantly. Today color cameras can be purchased at a price far below that which simple black and white cameras cost a mere ten years ago! So, video technology is entirely within the financial scope of any law enforcement agency.

What to do with that technology, however, is an entirely different matter. Due to lack of literature in the field of television as it relates to law enforcement, little awareness about television's potential in this area is evident. Also, lack of specialized literature has resulted in few trained personnel who can operate such equipment. Thus, no meaningful programs exist that utilize television in a manner meaningful to law enforcement.

Surveys indicate that much video equipment was secluded in closets for many years, gathering dust, because either no one understood how to operate it or no one knew what to use it for. What helped video to "come out of the closet" was the burgeoning consumer interest in the new video technology. This interest has spurred the industry into high-gear research and production. The result has been a change from the old, cumbersome, complex, and expensive equipment of yesterday to the new, lightweight, simple-to-operate, and inexpensive equipment of today.

In order to treat the subject most effectively, the authors have divided the book into two parts. Part One provides a basic background in video technology and acquaints the reader with the variety of video equipment available today and the way it works. Supplementing the equipment data are suggestions and recommendations as to what equipment is necessary and what criteria should be used for its selection.

Part Two of this book provides the reader with a practical application of video technology in routine and essential law enforcement activities. Part Two suggests guidelines for the actual incorporation and use of video within the local department and for the establishment of a training program in the use of video.

Appendices and the Glossary are provided for reference and research.

CONTENTS

Preface .... *Page* v

Part One
UNDERSTANDING TELEVISION

Chapter
1. WHAT IS TELEVISION? An Overview 5
2. ASSESSING NEEDS 9
3. VIDEORECORDERS 13
4. CAMERAS 31
5. VIDEOTAPES 40
6. ACCESSORIES 45
7. LIGHTING 56
8. AUDIO 63
9. EDITING 70
10. TITLING 78
11. PROGRAM FORMATS AND SCRIPTING 81

Part Two
APPLYING TELEVISION

12. TRAINING THE OPERATOR 89
13. TAPING THE DRUNK DRIVER 97
14. SURVEILLANCE 116
15. DEPARTMENTAL TRAINING 123
16. TRAFFIC 128
17. TAPING OF MAJOR CRIME SCENES 132

18	TAPING OF CONFESSIONS		135
19	CLOSED-CIRCUIT TELEVISION		138
20	PUBLIC RELATIONS		142
21	OTHER USES OF VIDEOTAPE		145

Appendices

A	MAJOR MANUFACTURERS		151
B	TELEVISION RELEASE FORM		152
C	PROGRAM SCRIPT		153
D	VIDEOTAPE OPERATOR'S STATEMENT FORM		154
E	ARRESTING OFFICER'S STATEMENT FORM		156
F	CHAIN OF EVIDENCE WAIVER FORM		157

Glossary 159
Bibliography 167
Index 169

TELEVISION AND LAW ENFORCEMENT

Part One
UNDERSTANDING TELEVISION

Chapter 1

WHAT IS TELEVISION?
An Overview

Television—that most pervasive and persuasive of modern technologies, marked by rapid change and growth—is moving into a new era, an era of extraordinary sophistication and versatility, which promises to reshape our lives and our world. It is an electronic revolution of sorts, made possible by the marriage of television and computer technologies.

The word *television*, derived from its Greek (*tele*—distant) and Latin (*visio*—sight) roots, can literally be interpreted as sight from a distance. Very simply put, it works in this way: through a sophisticated system of electronics, television provides the capability of converting an image (focused on a special photoconductive plate within a camera) into electronic impulses, which can be sent through a wire or cable. These impulses, when fed into a receiver (television set), can then be electronically reconstituted into that same image.

Television is more than just an electronics system, however. It is a means of expression, as well as a vehicle for communication, and as such becomes a powerful tool for reaching other human beings.

The field of television can be divided into two categories determined by its means of transmission. First, there is *broadcast* television, which reaches the masses through broad-based airwave transmission of television signals. Second, there is *nonbroadcast TV*, which provides for the needs of individuals or specific-interest groups through controlled transmission techniques.

Traditionally, television has been a medium of the masses. We are most familiar with broadcast television because it has been with us for about thirty-seven years in a form similar to what exists today. During those years, it has been controlled, for the most part, by the broadcast networks, ABC, NBC, and CBS, who have been the major purveyors of news, information, and entertainment. These giants of broadcasting have actually shaped not only television but our perception of it as well. We have come to look upon the picture tube as a source of entertainment, placing our role in this dynamic medium as the passive viewer.

Broadcast television maintained a singular stronghold in the public arena for many years, mostly due to the public's lack of awareness of the medium's potential and due to the lack of varied and inexpensive television equipment. However, two developments came about that were to influence and eventually to alter the character of television.

The first of these developments occurred by necessity during the early 1950s. A problem had been recognized regarding the quality of the televised picture at locations distant from the transmission point. As a result, pictures in these areas, mostly suburban and rural, were terrible, marked by interference, ghosts, break up, or no picture at all. This problem was technological, related to the inability of the television tuner to pull in the channel with sufficient sensitivity to yield a good picture. Two solutions were developed in an attempt to overcome this problem.

The development of more sophisticated and expensive television antennae had only marginal success. For the most part, the picture quality was still unacceptable, and consumers did not want to bear the burden of the additional expense or the sight of large, unpleasant-looking contraptions invading the neighborhood, so a second solution was developed. Microwave relay stations were set up to intercept the broadcast signal. These relay stations electronically boosted the TV signal and then sent it directly into the homes of the local community via a cable. This system, a kind of community antenna system, was known as CATV, community antenna television, and was the forerunner of today's giant cable TV industry.

The second development took the form of advances in technology, which brought about less expensive and less bulky television equipment. Significant within these technological developments was the videotape recorder, a device that functioned much the same as an audiotape recorder, with the exception that it could record picture as well as sound. This breakthrough exploded throughout the television industry.

Armed with new technology, closed-circuit television systems (CCTV) developed. These systems utilize television cameras and monitors and were adaptable for surveillance. They are now installed in many locations needing security.

With the availability of television equipment at reasonable cost and with sufficient diversity, individuals, including CATV operators, businesses, and educational institutions, jumped into television, and thus was born the second type of TV, *nonbroadcast television*. As its name implied, nonbroadcast television was developed to serve that segment of the public which had a more direct, specific interest. It reached its audience not through airwave transmission to the public at large, as did broadcast TV, but rather through such controlled transmission techniques as direct cable, closed-circuit TV, projection television, and videotape presentation. Television now could be created and viewed almost anywhere, including classrooms, offices, and businesses.

The CATV operator even began to provide local programming tailored to its own community needs. This led to what is today known as local access television, which is a far cry from the national coverage we were accustomed to from broadcast TV. Industry, business, and education utilized the new television technology as a means of instruction and communication to increase sales, to demonstrate, to teach.

Today, we live in such a fast-paced, ever-expanding technological world that it is becoming increasingly more difficult for us to keep abreast of all the latest developments. As a result, our perception of television has changed. We can no longer embrace the "passive viewer" and "television as entertainment" concepts. Instead, we see television as a new and dynamic medium that is subject to constantly changing applications. Within a few years, television has evolved from an almost purely entertainment medium with passive viewers to a dynamic, interactive medium in which the viewer takes active part. Already, videorecorders, videodiscs, and computers are revolutionizing television—putting it to such novel and varied uses as game playing, interactive banking/shopping, time shifting, data bases, and computer-aided instruction. Thus, the television screen of today is not so much a surface upon which images are viewed as it is a surface upon which images are displayed for purposes of interaction or manipulation.

The future promises even more spectacular reshaping of our understanding and use of television through such electronic developments (some of which are already here) as the following: the supersmall, superflat TV, similar to the high quality and tiny portable audio cassette players; the Camcorder®, a video camera and recorder built into a single, hand-held unit; interactive television, such as is found in interactive video systems using videodisc or videorecorder technologies; two-way cable systems and Videotext® capabilities, allowing the viewer to get news and information or to do his banking and/or shopping; DBS (direct broadcast satellite), allowing the user to intercept signals from the numerous communications satellites circling the earth; and digital televisions that, thanks to computer technology, will reduce circuitry, increase TV life, and provide sharper, clearer pictures. Also coming up is HDTV, high definition television, a supersystem in which the picture's overall resolution (or amount of picture detail) is doubled, rivaling the quality of a 35 mm slide.

Television is, indeed, a growing and changing medium, growing and changing to meet the needs of every user in his own way.

Chapter 2

ASSESSING NEEDS

Today, thanks to rapid developments in the electronics industry, a diversity of top-notch video equipment is available to meet virtually everyone's needs, from the professional to the semiprofessional to the amateur. With this glut of equipment often comes confusion or difficulty in making a decision as to which equipment is needed and/or desirable for a particular purpose.

The following chapters have been designed to provide the reader with information about various types of television equipment and their uses and applications, but before that, this chapter will address an important issue, one that is at the root of a successful television operation and one that can save time, money, and a considerable amount of grief and headache. The issue of concern is what might be called a plan of action, which is a systematic method of getting involved with television. Unfortunately, to some the development of a television facility lacks a well-thought-out plan. As a result, such a facility may appear deceptively simple: buy the equipment needed and get to work. The result is, more often than not, added expense, improper, insufficient, or too much equipment, little satisfaction, and, above all, little use.

The better (and recommended) approach is to analyze needs and expectations first. The first step in that direction is to select an individual to be in charge of finding out about television and its possible incorporation into the local or regional law enforcement agency. The basis for selection of such an individual should be his interest and background in television. Today, more and more individuals have gained some experience and interest in television thanks to the abundance of new home videorecording equipment and prerecorded tapes. So, there should be little problem in finding someone within the agency who has the interest and/or the background to take charge of the project.

Once the individual has been selected, he should undertake an in-depth study. This study should answer questions such as the following:

1. *Exactly what use is planned for such a facility?* (a) Is the primary purpose of a television facility to produce commercial-quality public relations tapes? (b) Is it to develop some instructional demonstrations of various law enforcement procedures and/or equipment? (c) Is it to tape the drunk driver? (d) Is it for use as surveillance? (e) Is it to be used as training material for new personnel? It may be all of these, more than these, or only one or two of these. What matters is that the intended use of the television facility has been clearly established beforehand.

2. *Who will operate the equipment?* Obviously, if a television production capability were to be established, someone would have to operate the equipment. This would require time for training with the television equipment, reading, and perhaps college course work for the individual selected. More often than not, the individual selected to be in charge of the television facility can serve as the head of operations where the facility is large enough to warrant several crew members. However, in small facilities where a limited capability is needed, the individual in charge can assume such operational management himself.

3. *Where is the equipment to be installed?* Depending upon what use is planned for the television facility, space needs can vary from a closet large enough to store the equipment to a fully equipped studio.

4. *How is the equipment to be paid for?* Funding for such projects should be well thought out. Often, federal, state, or local grants are available to pay for all or part of such equipment when adequate documentation can be provided that such equipment will improve the efficiency of the agency. Also, a presentation of the potential of a television facility before the local governing bodies can result in additional budgetary appropriations.

5. *What equipment will be needed based upon the intended use of the facility?* It is important to remember that the equipment needed is determined solely upon the intended use of the television facility. If, for instance, an agency has decided to purchase television equipment for use in the taping of drunk drivers, then the equip-

ment can be minimal. However, if one of the stated uses of the facility were to produce public relations tapes for the community, then much more sophisticated equipment would be needed.

Ultimately, the individual in charge will condense the study into a series of goals and objectives that will dictate what equipment will be needed and to what uses it will be put. This formalized study can then serve as an official guideline for the agency in utilizing its facility. Some possible goals and objectives might include the following:

1a. (goal) To improve the public relations aspects of the local law enforcement agency.
1b. (objective) The police department will create and make available to the community videotapes dealing with various aspects of local law enforcement including traffic regulations, protection against home burglary, bicycle safety.

In the example, the goal is the overall aim at which efforts should be directed, even though it may never actually be attained. The sample objective is known as a performance objective, that is, it states what will be done (creation of videotapes) and how it will achieve the desired goal (make tapes available for public).

Goals and objectives can be simple and short or long and complicated. It depends upon the individual situation, but one thing to remember is that goals and objectives must be realistic. It is wise to avoid entering completely unattainble goals and objectives, such as, "to reduce the local break and entry rate to zero" or "to eliminate traffic accidents." While such goals and objectives may be noble and ideal, they are not realistic because their achievement is improbable.

Once goals and objectives have been established, the individual in charge can undertake a study of equipment that is currently available and its costs. The purchase of equipment should be determined, as stated previously, by the goals and objectives already agreed upon, rather than vice versa.

The gathering of information regarding equipment and costs is a relatively straightforward process, consisting mostly of contacting merchants or major equipment manufacturers for current models and prices. Also, seeking the counsel of someone knowledgeable in television equipment (a local TV station or cable TV facility, a local college or high school audiovisual department, a local merchant, or even an interested resident) can often help in making a decision. In all cases, goals and objectives must play a major role in shaping the type and quantity of equipment needed. Only the person in charge and his department can decide exactly what equipment is needed and what they want to do with it. The following chapters in this section of the book provide some basic background information about equipment, which should prove useful and serve as a starting point for getting into television.

Chapter 3

VIDEORECORDERS

One of the most indispensable pieces of equipment, which by its very nature warrants that it be included in any television system, is the videorecorder. This electronic device places impulses onto magnetic tape, much the same as an audiotape recorder. The videorecorder, however, records both pictures (video) and sound (audio) simultaneously. Depending upon the particular equipment, the videorecorder can have any number of additional features, making its use more flexible. Today there are two basic types of videorecorder: the *open reel recorder* and the *videocassette recorder* (VCR).

Open reel format recorders include two types: the professional 1-inch quad (quadruplex) recorder and the ½-inch helical-scan recorder. Equipment such as this uses a reel of videotape that is manually threaded through the tape path and then passed onto an empty spool at the other end, much like an audiotape recorder.

In the VCR format are included the ¾-inch U-matic® cassette recorder and the ½-inch Beta and VHS recorder. In this equipment, tape is housed in a plastic cassette. When inserted into the videorecorder, the tape is automatically threaded.

To date, several attempts at a compact videocassette (CVC) format using ¼-inch videotape have not fulfilled expectations. However, new possibilities in the form of a camera and recorder in one unit may yet signal hope for this ¼-inch system.

Although the professional 1-inch open reel system and the semiprofessional ¾-inch U-matic cassette system are out of the scope and purpose of this book (due to their relatively high costs and operational complexities), a brief discussion of these formats will prove informative.

The videorecorder has almost single-handedly pushed the television medium to new and extended lengths and has to a consider-

Figure 1. One-half-inch open reel and cassette format videorecorders. Shown (clockwise from left) are the VHS consumer videocassette recorder, open reel portable recorder with AC adaptor/color processor/battery charger, industrial VHS cassette recorder, black and white video camera for use with open reel portable unit.

able degree helped television to realize some of its potential, particularly in the areas of selective viewing, time shifting, and individualized programming.

Preserving television images on videotape was not always possible, however. If we were to examine television in its early years, during the late 1940s and early 1950s, we would find that the only way to preserve a television image was through a process known as a kinescope. In this system, the scanning beam gun of a television picture tube was focused directly upon 16 mm motion picture film, where it exposed that film photographically. The result? A 16 mm print of the television signal. Such trailblazing efforts as this were, at best, viewable. Their key role, however, was preserving early television in a photographic form, leaving for future generations a record of that era.

It was not until the mid-1950s that the first commercially usable videorecorder became available. This large, bulky, and relatively clumsy device was not only expensive but limited to black and white recording. When color videorecorders came along shortly thereafter, they, too, were embraced by the broadcast networks, but these machines were merely the forerunners of today's sleek, compact and sophisticated recorders whose quality, function, and flexibility allow an unprecedented level of technical and artistic achievement.

In the *open reel quad (quadruplex) format,* magnetic tape 1 inch in width is manually threaded from a full reel on the left through tape path guides and across four video heads onto a take-up reel at the right. When the equipment is activated, the video heads spin rapidly as the tape is transported horizontally across them. Depending upon the desired mode (play or record), the spinning heads either read information stored on the tape and convert it into appropriate impulses to yield a television image or receive information through sources such as the camera and convert those signals into impulses, which are imparted onto the magnetic tape.

This quad format is today virtually standard in the industry, providing reliable performance and high quality. The price tag on such equipment is beyond that of all but professional production facilities and communications networks. Also, such sophisticated equipment with high quality, high costs, and high operating expenses is neither needed nor recommended for the routine law enforcement agency facility.

The key to the future of nonbroadcast television was, however, lurking within the confines of electronics labs. There, an entirely new format was being developed loosely based upon the quad recorder. This new format, known as 3/4-inch U-matic boasted three important innovations. First, it utilized a tape width of 3/4-inch instead of 1 inch. This meant that equipment could be smaller, lighter, more compact, and less expensive. Second, the tape was encased in a plastic housing—a cassette. This eliminated the tedium of manual threading (as well as protecting the tape from handling and serving as a time-saving convenience). Third, it boasted a new recording system, known as slant track or helical scan recording. In this format, as opposed to the quad format, the 3/4-inch tape passes from the full side of the cassette to the empty side of the cassette by following a U-shaped path (hence the name U-matic), which leads it across two or four rapidly spinning video heads that are set at an angle to the tape movement. This azimuth recording technique allows more information to be stored on the tape, resulting in high quality. Recording equipment such as this is used in electronic news gathering (ENG) operations at the broadcast networks and is capable of high quality. The ¾-inch U-matics include decks and portable units. It should be noted here that U-matic cassettes are not interchangeable between deck and portable unit. Because of the smaller size and compactness of the portable unit, its tape cassettes are also correspondingly smaller, allowing it to handle only twenty-minute cassettes.

Figure 2. Color camera with ¾-inch portable videocassette recorder.

Since the basic functions and features of the ¾-inch U-matic videorecorders are similar to that of its diminutive sister ½-inch format, an in-depth discussion of which follows shortly, and because the costs of the ¾-inch format make it generally prohibitive for all but large and well-budgeted agencies, this format, as well, is not necessary for routine law enforcement television production and is not within the scope of this book.

OPEN REEL ½-INCH FORMAT

While the 1-inch quad format and the ¾-inch U-matic cassette format fulfilled the needs of many in the communications field, there was still a group of potential users—small institutions, agencies, and businesses—for whom such professional-standard formats were both too expensive and too complex. Thus, another format, still smaller than the ¾-inch cassettes, was developed. This format, now standardized, is known as the ½-inch open reel or EIAJ format (Electronics Industries Association of Japan). This format was the workhorse and mainstay of video work when it was introduced during the late 1960s.

This standardized open reel system follows a format similar to ¾-inch cassettes in terms of its helical-scan and rotary-head system. However, in this case, the tape is only ½ inch in width and the open reels require manual threading, similar to a reel-to-reel audiotape recorder. While some compromises had to be made with the ½-inch format (picture quality was lower than the ¾-inch system, manual threading was time consuming and not always error free, recorders were limited to one hour recording in black and white for the first several years, lack of built-in tuning equipment prevented off-the-air recording, equipment was bulky and heavy), it nevertheless offered some significant plusses. The biggest plus came in the form of lower price tags and lower operating costs, making it an attractive buy for institutions, businesses, schools, and other local agencies.

Also, the development of the portable unit, the Portpak®, made a significant contribution to the longevity and utility of this format. Armed with camera, recorder, tape, and battery, the user could tape pictures and sound virtually anywhere and play them back later through the portable unit or from a deck. Another plus was the availability of inexpensive editing decks, allowing flexibility of programming.

Coupled with its standardization in the United States through the Electronics Industries Association of Japan (EIAJ), making any tape playable on any machine in this same format, such equipment made rapid inroads at schools, colleges, small businesses, and industries. The large quantity of such equipment that was purchased and subsequently utilized by these institutions has made it as much a part of everyday routine equipment as the 16 mm projector. Such extensive use of the ½-inch open reel EIAJ format has played a significant role in insuring its longevity. Although today it is being replaced by the newer ½-inch cassette system (discussed later in this chapter), the ½-inch open reel format is still in considerable use and will be for some time to come.

Within the vast diversity of ½-inch open reel equipment available, three basic and similarly functioning units can be discerned. Although minor variations may be present among various brand names, most recorders of this format share the same basic functions.

The standard deck, such as the Sony® AV-3600®, is a basic monochrome videorecording instrument, operating on alternating current, designed to preserve video and audio on videotape. Although its features are minimal and its picture is only black and white and limited to sixty minutes of recording, such a unit can suffice in many situations. The standard video deck incorporates basic features common to most videotape recorders, including stop, pause, play, fast forward, and rewind.

This deck, as with other videorecorders, houses two separate magnetic heads. They will be discussed in the order that the tape passes across them. The erase head is a full-track head that erases, or clears, everything from the tape. The next head is the video head. Actually, the video head is a complex assembly consisting of two or four video heads mounted on a rotating platform, which spins at high speed when the recorder is activated. This head assembly is located in the cylindrical drumlike unit—a visually prominent feature on the deck.

The next head is an audio/control head. The top part of the head places audio (sound) signals on the audio track of the videotape. The bottom part of the head is a control head. This part of the head imparts an electronic code to the bottom, or control, track of the tape.

The video heads are only part of the equipment of the videorecorder. There are also buttons and switches to provide ease of handling and optimum performance. These features include the following (from left to right on the recorder):

1. *The skew control knob* adjusts the tension on the supply reel so that it is uniform. Adjustment of this knob by turning it either left or right can alleviate some picture problems, particularly that of flagging or picture waving at the top. The tracking control knob adjusts the tape path to allow tapes from different units to be played with no compromise in picture quality.

2. *The tape counter* registers numerically to facilitate locating selected portions of a tape. The counter does not note amount of tape passed, nor does it denote the amount of elapsed time. Rather, it provides a continuous (up to 999) numerical increment for convenience in locating tape portions.

3. *The record button,* usually in red, cannot be activated by itself. It must operate in conjunction with the play button or lever. This feature protects the tape from inadvertent recording. Thus, to make a recording, *both* the record button and the play button (or lever) must be depressed simultaneously. The power switch turns on the main power to the unit. The selector lever or push buttons control actual tape movement in one of five modes: stop, rewind, play, pause, and fast forward.

4. *A camera/line switch,* located on the top panel in the example, is positioned relative to the type of input the operator is using. If he is working with a camera, the switch should be in *camera* position. If he is recording directly from a TV monitor, tuner, or prerecorded tape, the switch should be in the *line* position. Playback is not affected by the position of this switch.

5. *An audio dub button* may also be present on the standard deck. This button, when depressed, allows the user to erase and rerecord new audio information without affecting the existing picture.

All of these features are shown in Figure 3.

In general, the rear panel of such units includes similar features including the power-in cord, a separate outlet, video line input and output, camera input, 10-pin input/output, audio input for mike and line, and RF output.

The video line input accepts a direct video (picture only) signal and is useful for tape duplication. The camera receptacle allows the user to connect a video camera to the recorder. The 8-pin

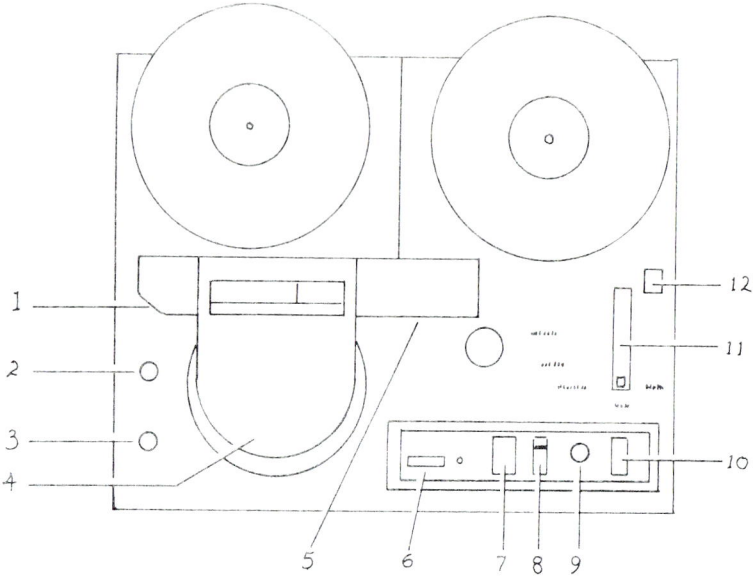

Figure 3. Top view of Sony AV-3600 video deck: (1) erase head, (2) skew control, (3) tracking control, (4) video head drum assembly, (5) audio/control head, (6) tape counter, (7) record button, (8) audio dub button, (9) audio agc/manual control, (10) AC power switch, (11) function lever, (12) camera/line switch.

connector allows the user to connect a monitor directly to the recorder for picture and sound information. An audio mike input allows for the connection of a microphone while the audio line input provides for direct sound from another recorder, records, tapes, and so forth.

The RF output requires an RF adaptor unit, a small electronic device that converts the video and audio television signals into frequencies that can be sent directly through the antennae of any television receiver. Since RF adaptors function on one of two unassigned local channels (usually channels three or four), the TV receiver should be tuned to this channel to receive the picture.

To play a recording, the operator should turn the power on. The deck should be properly threaded with recorded tape and the tape counter set at zero. To view the picture on a monitor, either the 8-pin connector or the video and audio line outputs from the recorder should be appropriately connected to the monitor.

In using a standard television receiver, the operator should be sure an RF unit is installed in the recorder. The RF output should be connected to the antenna terminals of the television set and tuned to the appropriate channel. Then the selector lever should be turned to play.

The tape will be transported from the left to the right reel, and the picture will be viewable after about three to six seconds. It takes about that number of seconds for the recorder to operate "up to speed."

In playing back a tape for future reference or editing, it would be wise at this point to make written notes relative to the picture content and the tape counter numbers. This will assure ease in locating recorded sections at a future time and will also be valuable for inventory purposes.

Recording a picture is nearly as simple. To record a picture, the camera (or line) input should be connected to the appropriate receptacle on the rear panel with the camera/line switch appropriately set. The television monitor or receiver should be properly hooked up (as explained previously). With the tape properly threaded and the tape counter set to zero, the operator should press the record button and hold it down while turning the function lever to play. Information coming into the recorder from the camera or line source will then be electronically recorded on the tape. Inasmuch as this basic deck automatically adjusts the picture and sound levels for best results, no further attention is needed.

As the tape rolls, it is good practice to make notes of content and tape counter numbers to facilitate later playback for viewing and/or editing and inventory purposes. A sample approach is as follows:

Counter Subject
000 — traffic survey
659 — drunk driving test
1090 — use of computer demo

As mentioned previously, this approach assures not only subject content of tape but full use of tape as well.

Features such as on/off switch, a mode selector lever or keyboard push buttons that include provisions for stop, play, pause, fast forward, and rewind are standard.

A deck such as this is not really capable of television production because it offers no facility for editing. Its main function is to provide straightforward record and/or playback capability.

A variation of such a deck comes in the form of a time-lapse recorder, one that has the capability of recording images in controllable time segments in order to condense, and thus speed up to a considerable degree, events that would normally take many hours. Such time-lapse equipment has surveillance applications in places such as banks.

There are, however, open reel decks with greater sophistication. These decks do allow a degree of electronic editing. An example is the Sony AV-3650®, a deck similar to the one just discussed. This deck allows for the simplest type of electronic editing, known as *assemble edit* (see Chapter 9). In addition, this deck has other features including automatic gain control (AGC) facilities for both video and audio, allowing automatic control of picture and sound levels. The deck also has manual override for these features, allowing the user to control picture and sound levels with his own touch. Variable slow motion is another feature providing frame-by-frame picture advance from slow to fast. This slow motion feature, not always available on decks, produces noticeable flicker during frame change.

Briefly, to make an assemble edit, the tape is placed in playback mode. An edit button located adjacent to the record button is depressed. When the point on the tape where the new material is to be inserted is reached (by examining the picture on the monitor), the operator simply depresses the record button and an electronic edit is made, placing the new material in that spot and erasing the previous material.

As stated previously, an editing deck such as this performs the simplest type of editing—the assemble edit. For instances in which the operator wishes to insert new material in the middle of a tape while not disturbing the remainder of the tape, another type of edit, an *insert edit*, and another type of recorder are needed.

An example of such a recorder is the Sony AV-8650® electronic editing deck. This unit far surpasses the previous units in functions and capabilities, although its basic operating features are similar. The most significant difference between the AV-8650 and the others is that this unit will also record color. And, because of upgraded electronics, its picture quality tends to be superior. However, the marvelous feature of this deck is its sophisticated system of electronic editing, allowing the user to perform assemble and insert edits in video, audio, or both modes. This adds tremendous flexibility and potential in video productions. (See Chapter 9 for further information about editing.)

Figure 4. A fully functional ½-inch open reel format electronic editing deck, the Sony AV-8650.

Versatility such as is found in this editing deck provides the potential for full production capability.

Portable Units

No greater impact was made upon videotape recording than the advent of the portable unit. This indispensable piece of equipment provides the capability of taping virtually anywhere. The portable equipment includes a lightweight recorder, a battery pack, and a portable camera. The typical portable pack will operate for up to one hour on a battery, although it can only handle thirty-minute reels of tape at a time. Recharging is simply accomplished by plugging the recorder's recharge unit into an AC outlet for up to eight hours. Coupled with an electronic-viewfinder portable camera, the portable pack allows the operator to view the tape immediately after taping.

Some portable units have outputs for video and audio as well as an RF output for viewing the picture on a television receiver. These units also have inputs for camera and line (usually a tuner).

Portable open reel units are available in both black and white and color. For users of color portables, a separate color processor accessory (which is included in the original purchase) is required in order to play a color picture through a color monitor or TV receiver. This color processor unit also serves as the portable unit's battery charger. Of course, color pictures require a color camera, which is an optional accessory.

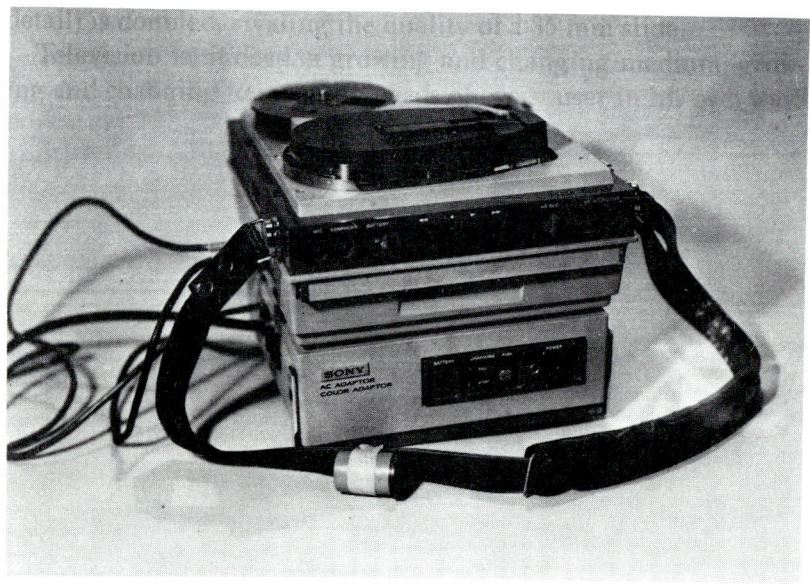

Figure 5. Sony ½-inch open reel format color portable videorecorder, shown with accompanying color processor/AC adaptor/battery charger.

On black and white models, a separate AC adaptor/battery charger can be purchased as an additional accessory.

Some portable units also offer automatic threading, an edit-pause mode (which causes the tape to back up slightly when the camera's record button is pressed, thus eliminating the usual glitch, or picture breakup, that occurs), and a numerical counter that registers increments in minutes. Any of these lightweight and reliable portables is a worthwhile addition to any video system.

The versatility afforded the user by the portable equipment is almost limitless. Coupled with an editing deck, a department can be well on its way to production capability.

VHS–BETA CASSETTE RECORDERS

The advent of the 1/2-inch videocassette recorder in Beta and VHS formats has pushed the medium of video to extended lengths. A combination of factors—price, ease of operation, availability of blank and prerecorded tapes, most wanted features, and a tremendous diversity of accessory equipment—have made these new 1/2-inch videocassette formats popular with both public and industrial users.

There are currently two videorecording systems in the half-inch cassette market. These include the Beta system, developed by Sony, and the VHS system (Video Home System), developed by JVC. While each system offers virtually comparable quality, differences in tape transport, threading, and recording, plus a small difference in cassette size, make the two systems totally incompatible. Thus, a tape recorded on a Beta format machine will not play on a VHS unit, and vice versa. However, cameras and accessory equipment are generally interchangeable between systems.

VHS and BETA systems have burgeoned relatively recently. Now there is the VHS–C® format, the ultramini cassette player (Fig. 8), and on its heels is the Super-8® video, a 1/4-inch camera/recorder in one, using a tape cassette slightly larger than a standard audiocassette.

The advantages of the VHS and Beta systems over standard open reel 1/2-inch videorecorders are significant. Loading and unloading a cassette recorder is much easier. The cassette is merely

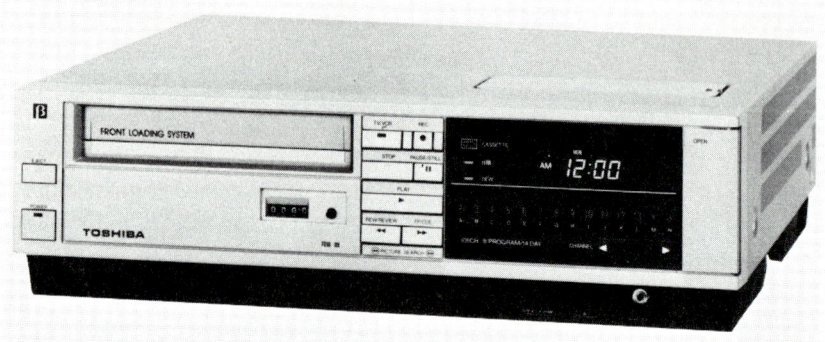

Figure 6. Beta format ½-inch cassette videorecording deck. Courtesy of Toshiba.

Figure 7. VHS format ½-inch cassette videorecording deck.

inserted into the loading device (either front or top load). The cassette also prevents touching or other contact with the tape. Such handling can have serious consequences, as residues and oils or other contaminants from the skin or other objects could cause defects in a recorded picture. Also, the cassette formats offer longer play/record modes, from one to as many as eight hours on a single cassette, and being somewhat smaller in size than open reels,

Figure 8. VHS–C format compact videocassette portable. Courtesy of Panasonic.

cassettes are more easily and compactly stored.

Both Beta and VHS systems offer similar features. In Beta, three tape speeds are known as Beta I, Beta II, and Beta III. Beta I, the fastest speed, is a playback speed only. Recording can be done in Beta II and Beta III speeds, which roughly correspond to the VHS SP and LP modes. VHS, however, has an SLP (super long play) mode that Beta does not yet offer. This increases the recording time of a tape significantly (see Chapter 5).

Other features found on both systems include audio dub and video dub, for incorporating new audio or video material into a tape. Also, forward (and reverse) search modes offer the capability of viewing the taped image at many times faster than the normal speed. Such a feature is useful in locating particular segments of a recording tape quickly. Slow motion and two and four times the normal speed also offer versatility and flicker-free images.

Both systems offer the advantage of industrial or consumer versions of their equipment. Industrial versions are made to withstand more wear than are consumer versions. However, most industrial versions do not offer the variety of features found on consumer models.

Another feature with both systems is remote control. With this option, recorders can be controlled via infrared waves (no connecting wires) to engage most of the recorder's capabilities from changing channels to recording and searching.

Perhaps the most significant advantage of the ½-inch cassette systems is their built-in tuner (many cable ready). This allows the unit to record off the air (or cable) directly with no additional hardware, as is the case with ½-inch open reel format units.

The ½-inch videocassette field also offers many portable units that are capable of performing the same functions as their AC counterparts. Portable units, which operate on battery power for up to one hour, when coupled with a portable color camera provide versatility, compactness, and mobility. The portable unit can serve as an essential part of any video production.

Maintenance

After many hours of recording, video heads develop a buildup of oxide particles from the tape. This condition, known as dirty heads, can severely and adversely affect the unit's performance, causing poor picture quality. If so much buildup occurs that the heads completely clog, then no picture will result. The best method of preventing this problem is through care in the use of the equipment and routine maintenance.

The operator can perform some routine maintenance himself.

Figure 9. Beta format portable cassette recorder, shown with accompanying tuner/time/charger. Courtesy of Toshiba.

Routine maintenance includes periodic dusting, checking the integrity of the case, and cleaning the video heads and other heads. Special head-cleaning cassettes are available, which make head cleaning relatively simple and trouble free. The head-cleaning cassette is inserted into the videocassette recorder just as any tape is. Only nonabrasive head cleaners (such as those using fluid and a chamoislike material) should be used, and their use should be limited. Excessive use of such cleaners can result in rapid head wear and can decrease overall head life dramatically.

Regardless of whether a head-cleaning cassette is used and whether routine maintenance is performed, equipment should be checked at least once a year for overall maintenance by a qualified service person. The equipment should be cleaned, both inside and out. Belts, gears, alignments, and heads should be checked. This will insure that equipment will be ready to perform when needed.

Chapter 4

CAMERAS

The television camera is the eye of the television system. It is an electronic instrument that is capable of transforming an image focused through its lens onto a pickup tube within the camera into a series of electrical impulses. These impulses can then be sent into a television set for display or into a videorecorder for preservation.

Depending upon the type of pickup tube within the camera, its sensitivity and picture characteristics will vary. Four basic television pickup tubes are currently available: the vidicon, plumbicon, newvicon, and saticon. Generally, speaking, vidicon tubes are less sensitive to light than the remaining three. Thus, such cameras will not operate well under very low lighting conditions but should prove entirely adequate for most studio/instructional applications. One of the inherent dangers with the vidicon tube, which is also the case to some degree with all TV pickup tubes, is its disposition to develop burn-in. This occurs when the camera is aimed for long periods of time at bright light or for short durations at the light source itself, such as the sun or photo lamps. It is important to be careful when aiming a television camera of this type, as burn-in will cause permanent damage to the pickup tube, resulting in a black spot or mark that will appear on any future picture recorded with that camera.

Plumbicon tubes are more light sensitive than vidicon tubes but also have what is known as a lag. This phenomenon causes very bright areas in a picture to smear when the camera is panned, or turned, towards another subject. Also, as is the case with the vidicon tube, this tube is subject to burn-in as well. Operators should use care and discretion when aiming television cameras with these tubes.

The saticon tube offers greater light sensitivity than the vidicon or plumbicon and offers less smear and less disposition to burn-in. It shares characteristics common to the newvicon pickup tube as well. Both are used extensively in today's color cameras. Because of their improved characteristics, these pickup tubes offer greater versatility in a variety of situations.

Several subdivisions can be made in camera equipment. (1) A camera can be a *studio* camera, a *portable* camera, or a *remote* camera, and (2) it can be a *monochrome* (black and white) camera or a *color* camera.

When nonbroadcast video equipment first became available, monochrome cameras were the standard item to go with them. Their relatively low cost, availability, and high quality made them ideal for low-budget black and white productions, especially in the ½-inch open reel monochrome videorecorder market.

Color cameras were not generally available in this nonbroadcast

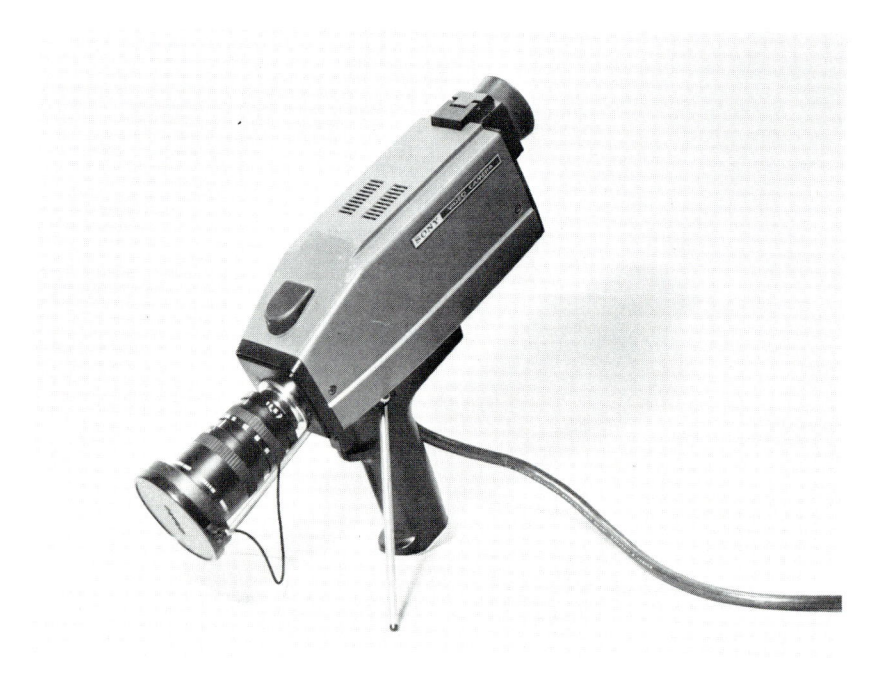

Figure 10. Standard black and white portable video camera with electronic viewfinder shown with zoom lens and built-in stand.

market except those with very high price tags. As a result, many video users worked with black and white cameras and recorders. Studio cameras were designed to operate on alternating current within a studio environment, and portable cameras were designed to operate on battery power to make them useful for field work. Remote cameras were designed for installation at locations distant from a monitor or recorder and served to meet surveillance and security needs.

As technology improved, however, color cameras became more accessible. This was due, in part, to the greater availability of color videorecording equipment and to the constantly lowering price tags of color cameras. Today, color cameras are available at costs equal to or even lower than the price of average-quality black and white cameras of ten years ago.

While there are significant differences between monochrome and color cameras in terms of their electronics, they share certain features or have such features available to make their use more effective and appropriate to particular needs. The type of viewfinder system is one of the distinguishing characteristics of a video camera. Cameras, whether monochrome or color, can incorporate one of two viewfinder systems. On less expensive cameras, an optical viewfinder system is used. This system, similar to that on inexpensive photographic cameras, provides a separate lens viewing system for composing the picture. Such viewfinders provide an inexpensive means of viewing the image while taking the picture. While more expensive optical viewfinder cameras may utilize an autofocus device that insures picture clarity with little effort on the operator's part, the less expensive optical viewfinder systems rely upon a manual focusing system in which a split image must be aligned. Focusing is achieved by rotating the focus ring on the lens while looking through the viewfinder. When the split image aligns itself, the camera is in focus.

One of the problems with optical viewfinders is a phenomenon known as parallax. Simply put, this means that what the camera lens (which is taking the picture) sees is slightly different than what the viewfinder lens sees. This is due to the difference in placement of each of these lenses. In videotaping critically aligned areas at close range, the operator should be aware of the probability that the image composed in the viewfinder will not be what the camera's lens sends to the television set or videorecorder. Edges may be missing and/or unwanted parts may be included.

This parallax problem is magnified somewhat because transmission of television signals to TV receivers results in the loss of part of the picture's outer edges. This portion of the picture is known as the *scanning area*. To insure that important parts of the televised picture are not lost, they should be framed well within the frame of the camera's viewfinder in what is known as the *essential area*. This will insure that important parts of the picture will remain intact when when the image is displayed on a TV set.

The second type of viewfinder system is the electronic viewfinder. In this system, a miniature television screen serves as the viewfinder, and as the operator looks into this tiny screen, he sees the actual television image that the camera is seeing. Consideration for essential picture area must also be taken into account with such electronic viewfinders. Whether the camera is monochrome or color, the viewfinder image is always in black and white.

Since cameras are designed to see images, they all need some kind of lens to take an image and focus it within the camera.

Figure 11. Portable color camera with electronic viewfinders shown with zoom lens and built-in microphone. Courtesy of Panasonic.

Figure 12. Another style of portable color camera with electronic viewfinder, zoom lens, and microphone.

Lenses perform two important functions. First, they allow an image to be focused (or made clear), and second, they allow control over the amount of light that passes through the lens, known as the f-stop (or aperture).

Two basic lens types can be distinguished. They include (1) the fixed focal length, or prime, lens and (2) the zoom lens. Fixed focal length or prime lenses are those whose field of view is preset to see a certain amount and nothing more. Such lenses are referred to by their focusing distance (to the light-sensitive screen within the camera) in millimeters. Prime lenses can be categorized into three basic focal lengths. They include the wide-angle lens, which sees much more than the human eye does. Wide-angle lenses usually have focal lengths under 20 mm and range from moderate wide angle to extreme wide angle (as in a fish-eye lens).

Lenses that see almost the same field of view as the human eye are known as normal lenses, and their focal lengths range from 20 to 30 mm.

Figure 13. Ultracompact and ultrasensitive surveillance camera. Courtesy of Sony.

The telephoto lens is one whose focal length ranges above 30 mm to 1,000 mm or more. These lenses make an image appear closer (actually, such lenses merely enlarge the image when it is focused on the photosensitive screen within the camera).

Along with the various focal lengths of lenses come other related factors, the two most important of which are perspective and depth of field. When a normal 25 mm lens is used, the image appears normal to the human eye. However, when a wide-angle lens is used, images become altered. Vertical lines seem to slant and converge, noses on faces appear somewhat larger, backgrounds appear more distant. The opposite is true of telephoto lenses. With such lenses, images appear to be flattened and compressed, with foreground and background appearing close together.

Depth of field also plays a significant part in the viewed image. Depth of field is an optical concept that refers to the amount of distance in front of and behind the focused object that appears clear. As the f-stop (or lens aperture) control on the lens barrel is turned from its widest opening to its smallest opening, more and more of the background appears in focus. As the lens aperture is opened to its limit, less and less of the background appears in focus. While wide-angle lenses extend depth of field considerably, telephoto lenses reduce it drastically.

Prime lenses may be permanently fixed to a camera (as may be the case with CCTV surveillance equipment), or they may be interchangeable by use of a lens mount. The C mount is a generally standard lens mount for both 16 mm cameras and video cameras within the scope of the 1/2-inch video format. There are, of course, always exceptions.

Many of today's newer cameras come equipped with a permanently affixed lens of variable focal length, known as a *zoom* lens. This lens, which incorporates the various characteristics of many prime lenses into a single unit, allows the user to magnify the image continuously while taping in order to achieve a look of moving in on the subject.

Whenever a camera is being used to record some sort of picture, the problem of camera technique becomes apparent. How does one handle the camera for maximum effect? What are some of the basic camera techniques that can be used in television?

As in motion pictures, television cameras share certain common techniques. Among them are techniques such as the pan (slowly turning the camera from left to right), dolly (slowly moving the camera in towards the subject), boom shot (raising or lowering the camera relative to the ground), zoom (using the special zoom lens to achieve effects similar to but not exactly the same as that achieved with a dolly), tilt (aiming the camera up or down), and tracking (allowing the camera to follow action by moving along with it).

In addition, good camera technique calls for steady camera handling and proper focus. Tripods are necessary in most instances for steady pictures. However, for those who are experienced in handling a camera, a hand-held shot with portable

Figure 14. Zoom lens mounted on color camera.

equipment is certainly feasible and many times desirable, inasmuch as it frees the cameraman from one position.

Another problem not as easily solved as camera technique is that of picture composition. Although many people may not be artists when it comes to dealing with pictorial space, there are certain commonsense rules regarding picture composition that will make viewing the tape not only informative but pleasing as well. As with all cameras, the television camera allows the user to select what he wants included in the picture, but a television camera can do more than that. With the proper cameraman behind the lens, it can emphasize or objectify certain pictures for dramatic or realistic effect. Selective focusing, camera proximity to the subject, and height of the camera all play a part in the manner in which the picture will be interpreted and understood by the viewer.

Care must be taken not to slant a picture inadvertently so that it produces the wrong effect. This can happen if, for instance, a drunk driver is being taped and the camera angle is very low. This may give the impression of a tall — perhaps menacing — individual. On the other hand, a high camera level may give the impression of a small, timid, and weak individual. Such slips in camera composition can create interpretive havoc. Selecting standard camera levels and angles, such as is done with mug shots, will eliminate such problems.

Other commonsense thoughts about composition include keeping the important visual information well within the essential area of the picture, maintaining the camera angle relatively horizontal, avoiding cutting off people's heads unless they must specifically be left out of the picture for ID reasons, and selecting appropriate lenses carefully.

As with all video equipment, the camera should be properly maintained. This is especially important inasmuch as the camera is so critical to the taping of images. Thus, when handling cameras, care also should be taken to avoid unnecessary shocks, as may happen if the camera is dropped or banged around during transit. Special cases with foam-rubber material are available, and they can prevent such damage to the delicate video camera.

Care should also be used in aiming the camera. As stated previously, the camera's pickup tube is susceptible to burn-in, and if it is aimed for even brief periods of time at bright light sources, the tube can be rendered useless.

Camera lenses should also be handled and maintained properly. Lens caps should cover the lens except when shooting. One should avoid touching the lens surface, and when cleaning, one should avoid scratching the lens. Use of a soft-haired brush to remove dust particles and use of lens tissue only when necessary will help prevent scratches.

Chapter 5

VIDEOTAPES

Videotape plays an integral role in the entire television process. It does this by providing a medium on which television signals may be preserved—a magnetically sensitive coating on a strip of plasticlike material.

If we were to examine videotape, we would find that it contains two sides. One, a dull charcoallike surface, is the backing material, much like the base of film. The other side, a shiny and smooth surface, is the oxide, or magnetically sensitive, surface upon which the actual recording is accomplished.

When a videorecording is made, the rapidly spinning video heads impart (or write) information on the moving videotape. They do this by creating a magnetic flux, a constant flow of variations in electromagnetic energy in direct relation to the incoming video impulses. These magnetic variations cause the magnetic particles on the tape surface, which is passing the heads with the most intimate contact, to be rearranged in such a way that they represent the magnetic variations being generated by the head itself. When the head is in a state of playback (or read), it detects, rather than creates, the magnetic variations on the tape and reestablishes the original magnetic variations. These are then changed into a series of electrical impulses that can be converted back into the original television signal and displayed for viewing.

Videotapes are distinguished by (1) format, (2) length, and (3) magnetic coating characteristics. In the open reel format, the videotape is wound (magnetically sensitive side always facing in) evenly and uniformly onto a reel. During playback, the take-up or empty reel should match the size of the supply reel to promote uniform playback and rewind. Open reel tapes are extremely vulnerable to damage, primarily because they are subject to handling by the user in threading the video unit. Handling the tape can play havoc not only with the tape but with the videorecorder as well, causing poor playback characteristics or dirty or clogged heads. Also, because such tapes are exposed to the atmosphere directly, particularly the edges (parts of which are exposed through the slots in the reel), the danger of dust contamination and other foreign matter is greatly increased. Thus, special care must be taken with open reel format tapes to prevent them from becoming unplayable. Such tapes should always be stored in their protective container and absolutely never touched.

Open reel format tapes come in a variety of lengths ranging from ten minutes to sixty minutes, including a five- and ten-minute endless-loop cartridge for repeated playback.

Open reel videotape also features a regular (normal) magnetic coating and a high-energy coating. High-energy tapes (similar to cassette's high grade tapes) improve overall picture characteristics by responding more favorably to the electronic impulses and by reducing the number of dropouts in the picture.

It should be noted that videotapes, whether open reel or cassette, are not playable on both sides, and users should not attempt to play or record a tape on both sides. In most cases, the reel or cartridge will not allow this anyway; however, if this is done, the front side information will be completely erased. It should also be noted that because the video signal is electronic and because this electronic signal carries picture information, including color, the same tape can be used for recording black and white or color (assuming a color videorecorder is available).

The VHS format offers a variety of ½-inch tapes housed in a plastic cassette, which not only protects the tape but provides for automatic threading. VHS format tapes range in length from a loop cassette for repeated playback to cassettes running in length from thirty minutes up to eight hours. Such tapes are designated by the letter T- plus the number of minutes the tape runs at VHS standard play mode. Thus, a T-30 tape plays for thirty minutes at SP, sixty minutes at LP, and ninety minutes at SLP. A T-120 tape plays a total of two hours at SP, four hours at LP, and six hours at SLP. Such tapes also come in standard and high grade types, the high grade offering somewhat improved picture quality, less dropouts, and higher signal-to-noise ratio.

Figure 15. Relative sizes of videotapes. From left to right, ¾-inch videocassette, ½-inch sixty-minute reel, ½-inch VHS cassette, ½-inch Beta cassette.

These tapes, however, have a higher price tag as well.

Relatively new to the VHS format is the VHS–C (C for compact) videocassette. These cassettes, designed for use in portable units, have a recording and/or playback time total of twenty minutes. Such cassettes cannot directly be played in a standard VHS deck. However, with the purchase of an additional collar device, such cassettes can be played in regular VHS decks with no problem. The VHS–C format was developed primarily to reduce size and increase compactness of portable units.

The Beta format also offers a variety of tapes similar to that of VHS. Beta cassettes are not playable on VHS units due to a different threading pattern and differences in the electronic recording characteristics. Beta cassettes are also somewhat smaller in size than the VHS type.

Beta format tapes cannot record in what is known as the Beta I speed (this is used only for playback). Beta II and III speeds correspond to VHS SP and LP modes. Because of the recording and time characteristics of the Beta system, its playing times approximate half that of VHS.

VIDEOTAPE INVENTORY CONTROL

It is important to maintain an accurate account of a department's videotape library, especially the proper and up-to-date indexing of subject matter, time, tape number, and counter numbers. Such an inventory makes the video library extremely useful. A nonexistent or poorly maintained index of videotapes makes the library highly unmanageable.

Each tape should always carry a label, both on the cassette itself and on the storage box. The label should include the tape number and some indication of subject(s). Tapes should be stored vertically in a cool, dry location away from strong magnetic fields.

When videotapes are recorded, any previous material is automatically erased. If this method is unsatisfactory, and a completely unrecorded tape is needed, the tape can be erased in one of two ways:

1. The tape can be erased by placing it in the recorder and recording with no incoming signal. This assures a completely clean video, audio, and control track. However, this method will tend to wear down the erase and video heads unnecessarily.
2. The tape can be erased using a bulk eraser of the type manufactured for each format tape. This device emits a strong magnetic field, which completely erases all magnetic information on the tape in a matter of seconds. This method is quick, efficient, and saves wear on the video and erase heads. It is important to select a bulk eraser of sufficient strength to do the job. Consult with the dealer regarding bulk eraser characteristics.

There may be times when a user wants to protect a videocassette from accidental erasure while it is in a recorder. This can be accomplished by removing a plastic tab on the cassette. Without this tab, the recorder cannot be placed in the record mode. If the user later wishes to record on a cassette from which the tab has been removed, he can simply place a piece of masking or cellophane tape across the opening where the tab was located. This will enable recording on the cassette.

By maintaining an updated tape library and following recommended handling and storage procedures, tapes should last indefinitely.

Chapter 6

ACCESSORIES

Without question, somewhere along the line in television work, the video operator will need some kind of accessory. It may be anything from a plug or an adaptor to a microphone mixer or special effects generator. This chapter will provide background information about the enormous variety of accessories that more often than not, can make or break a good production.

Plugs, Jacks, and Adaptors

One of the most common and frustrating accessory problems confronting the video user occurs when he attempts to interface a cable from one recording unit (or audiocassette deck or phonograph) to another device, and he finds that it does not fit. More likely than not, in such a situation the user can extricate himself from the dilemma through the use of accessories known as jacks, plugs, and adaptors. The following paragraphs will discuss the different types of jacks, plugs, and adaptors and the ways they may be used.

Jacks are those devices which serve as receptacles into which plugs are inserted. Adaptors are devices that modify the existing plugs, making them compatible with a different jack type. There are numerous jack, plug, and adaptor types, some for audio and some for video.

The most common audio plugs include the standard phono plug, the RCA plug, and the mini plug. Some industrial equipment and accessories may utilize a cannon connector. The common audio plugs are shown in Figure 16 in their relative sizes.

Adaptors for audio plugs are also available. One end of the adaptor is a jack of one type, and the other end is a plug of a different type. To use an adaptor, a user simply determines how he wants to convert the plug. For instance, if he has a cable with an

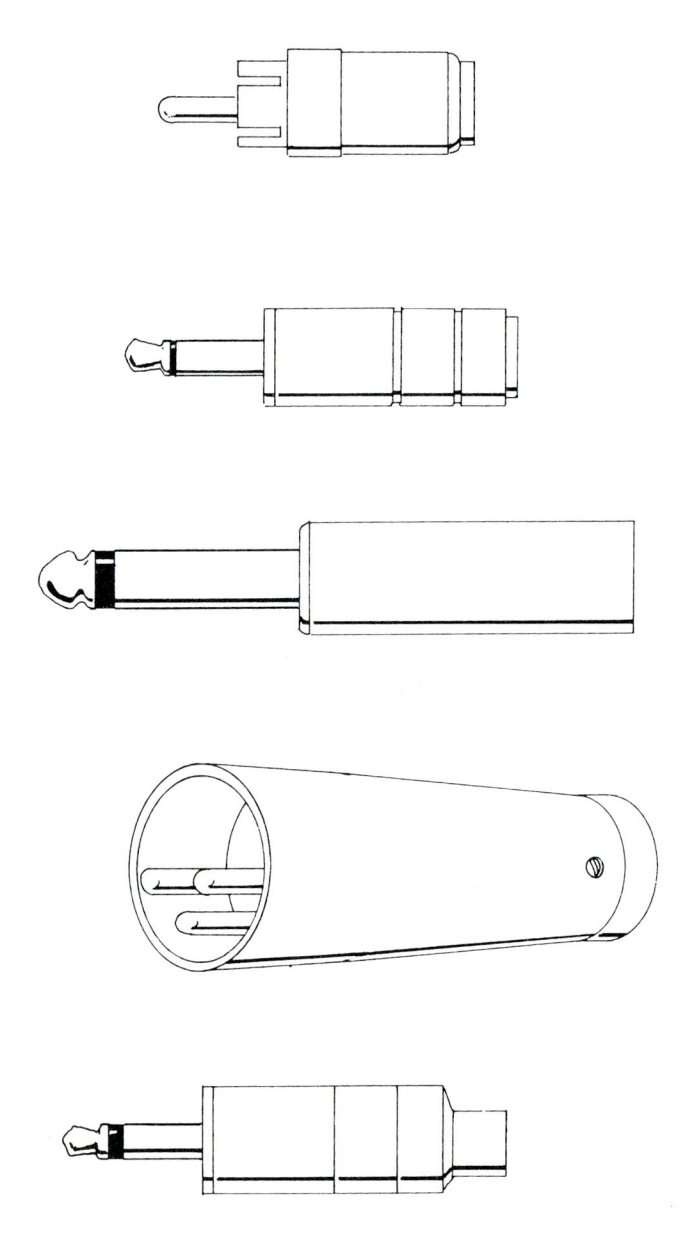

Figure 16. Common audio plugs shown in relative size. From top to bottom, RCA plug, mini plug, phono plug, cannon-plug, RCA to mini adaptor.

RCA plug that must be plugged into a videorecorder that has only a mini jack, he would use an adaptor that has an RCA jack at its back end and a mini plug at its front end. By inserting the RCA plug into the RCA jack of the adaptor, he has converted the plug from RCA to mini, and it can be readily plugged into the mini jack.

Adaptors allow for any number of combinations, such as RCA to mini, phono to mini, phono to RCA, RCA to phono, and so on. Such adaptors are among the most valuable of accessories because of the ease with which they allow on-the-spot connections to be made. A variety of video plugs also exist. Among the most common types are the UHF, BNC, 8 pin, 10 pin, RCA, and F-type.

Stopwatch

Another necessary item is a stopwatch. While many productions may not require it, a stopwatch comes in handy for editing purposes especially, where every second counts. Stopwatches can also help determine tape use while recording and/or battery life while recording.

Stopwatches are available in both the traditional spring-wound type, which may time in thirty- or sixty-minute modes or in the electronic LED type, with digital readouts.

RF Adaptor

Another accessory that can come in handy, mostly for open reel format users, is an RF adaptor. Designed to allow the videorecorder to interface with a regular television receiver, this device allows a recorded signal to pass into the television's antenna terminals so that the picture can be displayed when the set is tuned to a blank local channel corresponding to the frequency of the RF adaptor (usually channel three or four). Without such an adaptor, open reel users will require a genuine television monitor and will have to go directly to the video and audio inputs ($^1\!/_2$-inch cassette recorders come equipped with built-in RF adaptors). This has some advantage for production (picture clarity, full scanning image, greater picture control) but also has a disadvantage (higher costs).

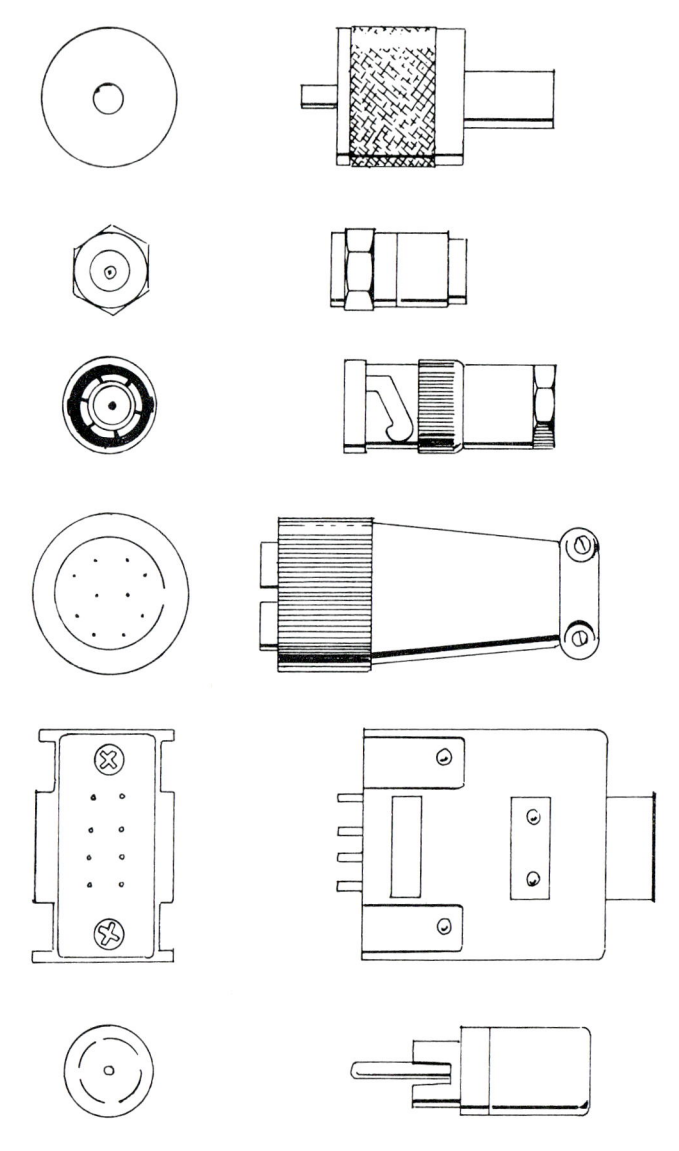

Figure 17. Common video plugs (front and side views) shown in relative size include (from top to bottom) UHF, F-type, BNC, 10 pin, 8 pin, RCA.

Tripod, Monopod, and Brace

Among the most necessary accessories is the tripod. This three-legged device supports and steadies the camera while taking a picture. Tripods come in a variety of types and sizes, with prices that range from less than $50 to more than $500. For general purposes, a tripod should have (1) adjustable legs so that it can be raised or lowered to various heights, (2) a pan head so that the camera can be turned left and right, and (3) a tilt head so that the camera can be aimed up or down. Some tripods have additional support in the form of a leg brace. In any case, to insure steady pictures a tripod should nearly always be used. A variation of the tripod is the monopod, a single-legged pole with a camera mount on the top. The monopod, while small and compact, does not offer the stability of a regular tripod.

In the absence of a tripod or as an alternative to one, a shoulder brace can be used. This device fits over the operator's shoulder and is balanced around his waist. The camera is attached to a mount at the top, and the brace supports the camera weight, freeing the operator's hands for aiming, focusing, and so forth.

Dollies

There may be times when the camera should be able to move, such as in a tracking shot or a dolly shot. In such cases, a device with wheels, which fits under the legs of a tripod, is necessary. This device, known as a dolly, allows the operator to move the camera freely in any direction with relative ease and smoothness. Some dollies have brakes to make them immobile so there is no inadvertent movement. Dollies should be used on relatively smooth surfaces such as linoleum or tile floors.

Camera Extension Cable

Sometimes the video user may want to move the camera farther from the recorder than the video cable will permit. Most portable video cameras come with relatively short cable lengths. To solve this problem, a camera cable extension cord is desirable. With such a cable, the user can increase the length of the camera cord to 25 or 50 feet. This solves many camera movement problems (but can also create some spaghettilike tangles when many cameras with extensions are used at one time and sprawl across a studio floor).

Mixers, Switchers, and Segs

Among the more useful of accessory equipment are the mixers for both audio and video.

Microphone Mixer

A relatively simple component, a microphone mixer is indispensable when more than one sound source is required. Such mixers allow the user to connect two (or more) microphones or other audio sources so that they can be mixed and manipulated with individual volume controls to produce the desired effect. Microphone mixers are a must for panel productions or dramatic presentations where sound effects and/or background music must be incorporated. A microphone mixer such as the one illustrated in Figure 18 allows four separate audio inputs, each with its own volume control. This unit also contains a master volume control unit with a volume meter (VU meter) for a controlled audio output. Some additional features of mike mixers include selection of high or low impedance sound sources, a battery-operation capability, and a test tone signal.

Camera Switcher

Perhaps the most glamorous of the mixers are those for television cameras. The simplest type of camera mixer is actually a camera switcher. This device enables the user to push a button in order to switch from camera one to camera two, for instance, but it does not allow both images to be mixed together on the screen at the same time. Passive camera switchers are purely mechanical devices. As such, they have a tendency to cause a slight glitch, or breakup in the picture, when a switch is made. More sophisticated camera switchers, known as active or electronic switchers, contain electronic components that provide for relatively glitch-free

Accessories 51

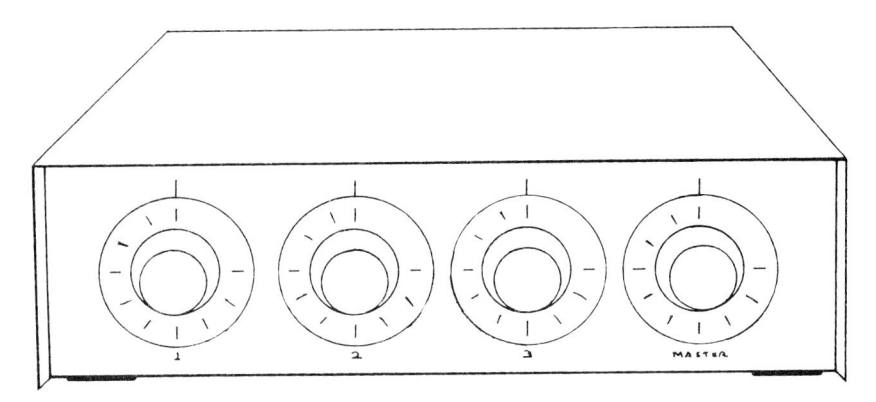

Figure 18. Typical microphone mixer allows several audio inputs to be mixed into a single output.

switching. Such switchers are relatively inexpensive and limited in effects they can produce.

SEGs (Special Effects Generator)

In order to obtain genuine mixes with cameras, sophisticated electronic systems must be employed that synchronize camera signals. Such mixing devices are actually known as SEGs, or special effects generators.

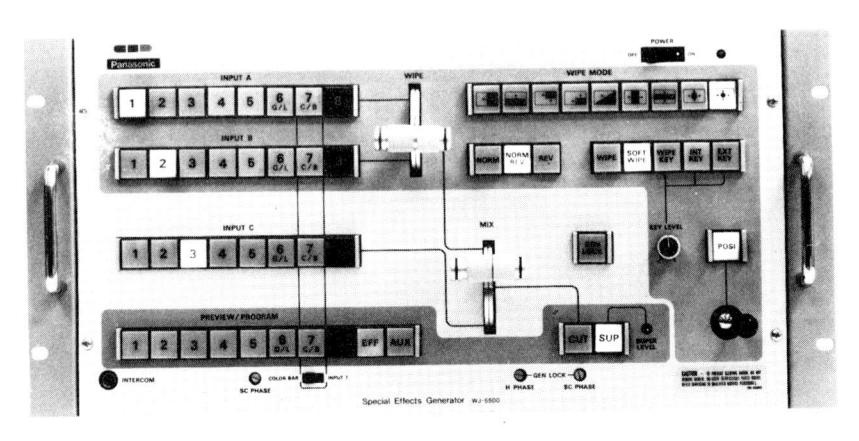

Figure 19. Deluxe color special effects generator allows for switching, mixing, and creating special effects. Courtesy of Panasonic.

While a special effects generator is not an editing device, it can aid in achieving editing through careful camera selection while production is being recorded. Genuine SEG devices synchronize and lock incoming video signals so they may freely be manipulated. Everything from superimposing to keying (inserting part of one picture into another) to fades, dissolves, and wipes can be achieved simply and professionally.

Monitors and Receivers

Monitors are television sets with special properties that make them different from regular television receivers. Monitors provide direct video and audio inputs without a tuner. This means that the signal travels directly to the display area and produces a quality that is clear and sharp. Also, because the image is going into the monitor directly, it provides a full scanning area picture (everything the camera sees is also seen on the monitor screen).

Television receivers, on the other hand, do not always provide as sharp and clear a picture, mostly due to transmission interference, which subtly erodes overall quality. Also, due to transmission, some of the picture area is lost along the outer edges. What results is known as the essential area. Parts of the picture that would be visible on a monitor are lost in the receiver, but this is usually satisfactory, since the outermost limits of the picture composition are by design meant to be insignificant. Television receivers are, in general, less expensive than genuine television monitors.

Battery Chargers

Although charging capability is normally a built-in feature of portable units, allowing the user to charge a depleted battery within two to eight hours, there are times when additional battery chargers may be needed to maintain several battery packs for anticipated extended recording. For this purpose, separate charging units are available.

Figure 20. VHS portable videorecorder (left) shown with accompanying AC adaptor/battery charger (right).

Signal Splitters

A television signal may at some time need to be seen at more than one location simultaneously within headquarters. To accommodate such a situation, a signal-splitting device is necessary. The signal splitter allows a primary video signal to be broken up into several separate signals, each fed to its own monitor/receiver. More sophisticated electronic splitters, such as distribution amplifiers, perform a similar function but at a greater range and with considerably more cost. For most purposes, a simple signal splitter will suffice.

Modulators

In the event a community is served by a cable television system that offers access channels, a user can, with the cooperation of the cable company, provide cable broadcast capability throughout the community to cable subscribers with an electronic unit known as a modulator. This device allows police departments to play one of their recorded videotapes (or live production) into the cable system, where it can be tuned in by subscribers. Such systems, in wide use today, offer a new outlet for dissemination of information and for public relations. Anyone interested in this system should check with his local cable company for specific details.

Crawls

Most people are probably familiar with the credit crawl at the end of a TV program or a movie. The names of those responsible for the production slowly and smoothly move up the screen. This is known as a crawl (in computer-generated credits, it may also be known as a scroll).

Although professional, sophisticated crawl devices, consisting of a variable-speed motor, a drum assembly, and capability for front or rear lighting are available at considerable expense, an amateur can achieve somewhat similar results by constructing his own crawl device at almost no cost. Supplies needed are a cardboard carton, perhaps 10 inches by 12 inches (or bigger), two wooden dowels slightly longer than the width of the box, a small crank handle (such as is found on jalousie windows), a roll of paper slightly narrower than the width of the box, and masking tape.

With a sharp instrument, one should make two dowel-diameter holes on the left and right sides of the box so that they are about 1 inch from the top edge of the box and about 2 inches from the front and back of the box (see Fig. 21). One dowel is inserted through the front hole so that it goes through the side of the box, across the box interior, and out the other side of the box. A roll of paper onto which names and other credits have been typed is taped to the cranked-dowel and the remainder is allowed to curl around the other dowel. One then simply turns the crank slowly to move the paper smoothly upwards and aims the camera straight down at the moving letters.

Accessories

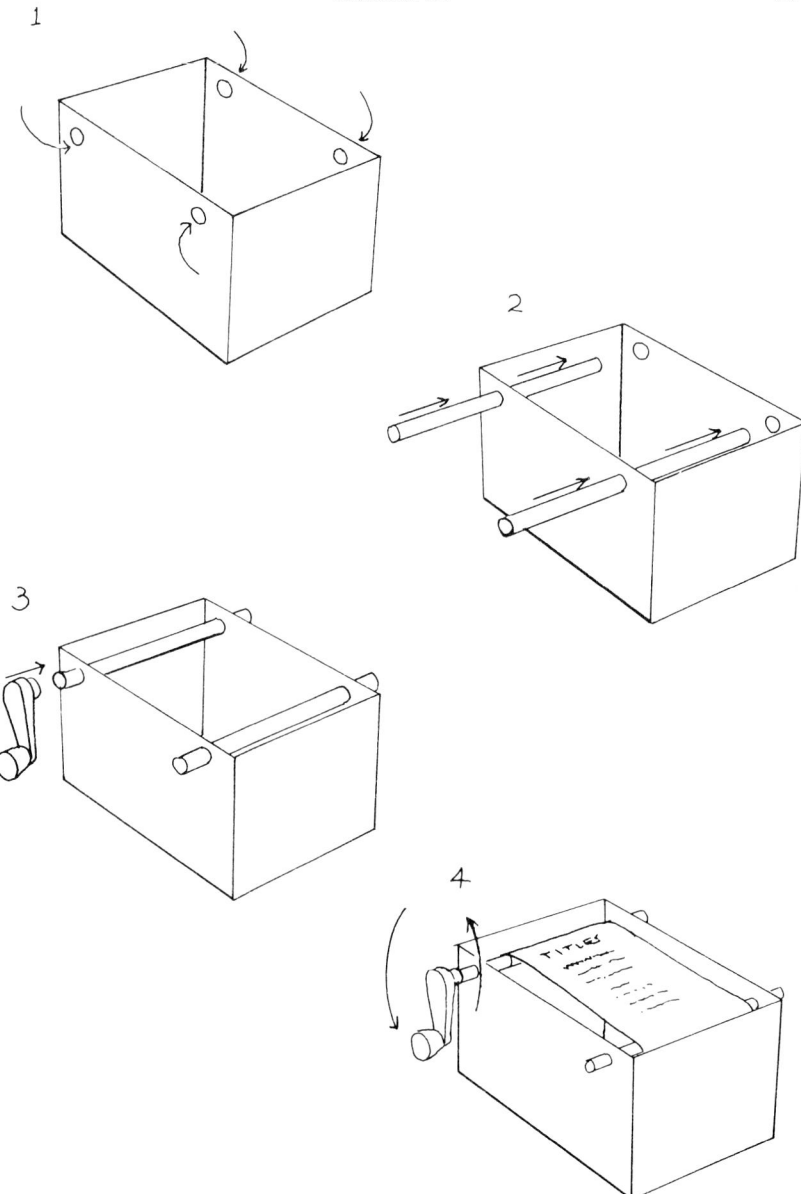

Figure 21. Construction of a crawl device. (1) Dowel-size holes are made at top corners of box. (2) Dowels are inserted through holes. (3) Handle is attached to the end of one dowel. (4) Paper with titles is taped to dowel with handle while remaining paper is draped over other dowel.

Chapter 7

LIGHTING

Lighting plays a significant role in all video productions. Light reveals the substance, appearance, and form of an object or surface by reflecting from a surface and into the lens of an image-recording device such as a camera.

Light, as we know it, is actually electromagnetic energy that travels in various wavelengths. Some of this energy falls within what we know as the visible spectrum—that portion of light energy which the human eye can see. Some of this energy falls beyond the visible spectrum and remains invisible to the human eye, such as X-rays or infrared radiation. In either case, however, such energy can be detected by various film emulsions and specially sensitized electronic plates within television cameras to allow a recording of an image to take place.

All of light can be divided into two basic sources. They are natural lighting, such as the sun, and artificial lighting, such as lamps, spotlights, bulbs, and so on. The television user will want to utilize both sources for maximum flexibility and impact. However, certain characteristics about each light source must first be understood. In this way, one can avoid common errors of judgment that can result in unusable pictures.

Light possesses a multitude of diverse characteristics, whether it is natural or artificial. Of concern to video users, however, are these four:

1. Light quality
2. Light direction
3. Light temperature
4. Light intensity

Light Quality

Light, whether it comes from the sun or from an artificial source of some sort, can provide a direct quality. Such direct lighting imparts a contrasty appearance to the subject. Perhaps its most characteristic feature is the sharply defined cast shadow it creates.

In direct lighting, which usually occurs in daylight on clear days but can also occur with the appropriate artificial light, human faces are characterized by deep, dark recesses where the eyes are and strong shadows beneath the nose and under the chin. Often such direct lighting causes the subject to squint.

Generally direct light scenes are marked by extreme contrasts. This means that some or all shadow or highlight detail may be lost. The problem is due to the limited range of gray-scale sensitivity most video cameras have. Thus, direct lighting is not always desirable. When conditions necessitate taping in direct light, it is advisable to soften that light with a reflector of some sort (a large white or silvered cardboard sheet or a large white sheet held near the subject so that the direct light source bounces off it and spreads more evenly, filling in any dark spots or harshness on the subject). Moving the subject into open shade can also help relieve the direct-light harshness.

In cases where direct lighting is being utilized for videotaping, care must be taken to avoid aiming the video camera so that the light source is within viewfinder range. Such a situation can not only cause lens flare (spots of light spreading throughout the picture due to its refraction in the lens) but also can damage the pickup tube and leave black burn-in spots as a permanent feature of that camera's recorded images.

Light, whether from the sun or an artificial source, can also be indirect, known as diffused lighting. Diffused light is characterized by an even, overall illumination and very soft, fuzzy-edged cast shadows. Sometimes diffused lighting is so extreme that no shadows are visible. Such diffused lighting tends to reduce overall contrast and soften the picture. In some cases, a picture may appear too flat, a condition in which the lighting fails to emphasize the three-dimensional character of an object.

Diffused-lighting effects can be achieved in daylight by shooting on a very hazy or cloudy day. Indoors, a multitude of artificial lights can be used to achieve the same effect.

Direct photofloodlights and spotlights can be diffused by placing a diffusion screen in front of the light source. A direct light source can also be aimed at a white or light-colored surface such as a wall or ceiling to bounce the light, thus causing it to diffuse.

Light Direction

Since birth, we have been conditioned to recognize images from a light source that comes from above—the sky and the sun. As a result, much of what we know visually has been determined by this lighting direction. It is most common and most familiar to us. However, light, particularly artificial light, can be controlled so that it comes from any direction. For the artist, such unusually directed lighting can serve to enhance the image and provide effect for emotional and intellectual impact. Such has been the case with mystery and horror films, in which low light levels serve to provide an unusual and often frightening image. In police work, however, lighting must in many instances be utilized for image recognition, as in the case of surveillance or testimony of some sort. Therefore, unless unusually directed lighting is needed for demonstrations purposes, simulations, or dramatic presentation, it should be directed from the place people are most accustomed to—above.

Light Temperature

If color photographs are taken indoors with outdoor film, there is a noticeable reddish cast to the prints, and a house lamp turned on during a sunny day may give off an orange-looking light when compared with sunlight. These subtle color shifts relate to what is known as the color temperature of the light source. Measured in degrees Kelvin, color temperature ranges from bluish-white to reddish-orange. Daylight, for instance, is approximately 5,400 degrees K, a 500-watt photoflood bulb approximates 3,400 degrees K, and a regular 100-watt household bulb approximates 2,900 degrees K.

Early in the morning and late in the afternoon, when the sun's angle to the earth decreases and the sun's energy must penetrate more of the atmosphere, many of its light wavelengths are absorbed, particularly in the blue end of the spectrum. As a result, the color quality of that light tends to be rosy or red or orange. At noon, however, when the sun is at its most direct angle, penetrating a minimum of earth's atmosphere, most of its light wavelengths can pass through, including the blues. The result is a color quality of bluish-white, known as daylight.

Since most color video cameras accommodate both types of color temperature through use of filters, proper color balance can be attained.

Light Intensity

Light intensity refers to the strength of the light source. The higher the intensity, the brighter the scene; the lower the intensity, the dimmer the scene. With sunlight, the intensity can vary due to time of day, clouds, haze, and shaded areas. With artificial lights, intensity can vary due to the type of light source used and its power or due to the distance between light source and subject. As the light source is increased, its illumination power diminishes.

One important consideration when dealing with varying degrees of light intensity is the correct lens setting (measured in f-stops). Some lenses have an auto-iris feature, which allows them to adjust automatically for a given amount of illumination. In such cases, the user merely aims the camera and shoots. However, if the light source is too intense or if the light source is too weak, the camera will fail to register an image that is usable.

In situations where too much light exists and the image becomes overexposed and washed out, a special light-reducing filter can be attached to the lens. This filter, a neutral density filter, available in varying degrees of light reduction, acts much like a pair of sunglasses and absorbs some of the light coming into it. Because it is neutral in color, it has no effect upon color rendition. Usually such filters are required if one is shooting against an extremely bright subject, particularly in sand or snow.

In cases where there is too little light, a camera will not register an image no matter how far open the lens is set. In such cases, the user will have to resort to artificial light. There may be times, however, when such artificial lights may be undesirable, such as during surveillance. In such cases, special light-sensitive cameras, sensitive to very low light levels, can be used. If that does not work, there is always the infrared sensitive camera, in which an infrared light source invisible to the human eye can be used for recording purposes.

Basic Lighting Concepts

When working under daylight conditions, a camera user can do little to modify the light source except to move into open shade or use reflector devices to diffuse the sunlight. However, when the user is working indoors with artificial lights, such as would be found in a studio situation, lighting can be completely controlled to suit the particular purpose. It is helpful, therefore, to discuss some very basic concepts of artificial lighting for television.

In most situations, a three-light setup is generally used. This classic approach to lighting, used for years by professional still photographers, has been borrowed by the film and television industry. The classic setup includes a primary light source, which serves to illuminate the subject while providing a revelation of three-dimensional form. This light, because it plays a key role in revealing basic form and structure of the subject, is known as the *key* light. Its placement is generally 45 degrees to the right or left of the subject and well above eye level. As the key light casts its glow in an angular direction, it provides a strong relief of form, reminiscent of a Rembrandt painting. The key is normally of great intensity.

A second light source, aimed primarily at filling in dark recesses caused by the direct light of the key, is known as the *fill* light. This light, a diffused light of relatively weak intensity is positioned alongside the camera and slightly above eye level. The fill light can serve also as a *base* light for television purposes. As such, it is designed to illuminate a set evenly to prevent excessive contrast.

In order to bring the subject into more relief and allow the

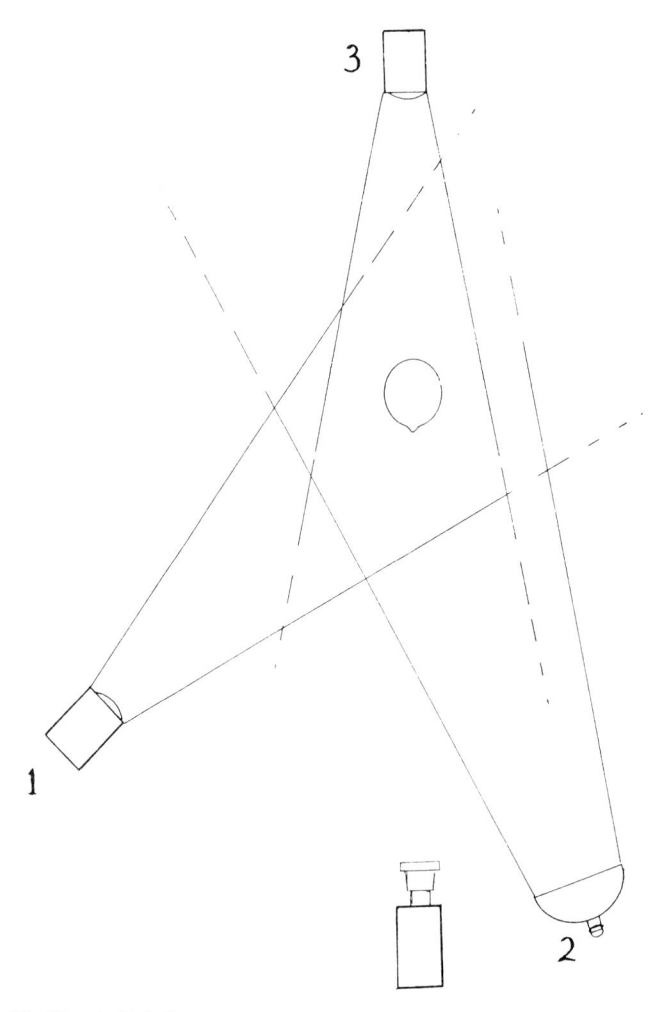

Figure 22. Classic lighting setup includes (1) key light, (2) fill light, and (3) back light.

picture to appear more lively, a third light, known as a *back* light is used. This light, also of great intensity, is positioned well above and behind the subject. Its light is cast down across the subject's head and shoulders, providing a bright separation between the subject and the background.

Lighting Accessories

For most indoor purposes, photoflood lamps, quartz-iodide lamps, and regular outdoor floodlights can be used as illumination sources for television production. Common needs in addition to the lamps and to the lamp housing include spare bulbs, diffusion screens or scrims, extension cords, gaffer tape (electrical grade masking tape), light stands, plus various reflectors. Reflectors can be parabolic or the barn-door type, which is actually a pair of movable flaps designed to control light output and, to some degree, light direction.

Chapter 8

AUDIO

Sound—an important ingredient in any video production—adds a degree of authenticity and realism to the image. Because sound plays such a key role in the credibility of any taped picture, its use should be considered a significant aspect of the final taped product.

If we examine the nature of sound, we find that it is a series of pressure waves dispersing through the atmosphere from a source. Unless our ears or some other device is set up to intercept and interpret these waves, they remain as mere pressure waves. Everyone has probably heard the old story about a tree falling in the woods. If no human or animal is around, does the tree make a sound as it falls? Technically, no. Sound is an interpretation made possible by the combination of the hearing apparatus and past experience of humans and animals.

There are, however, nonhuman/nonanimal electronic devices that can "hear" sound. These devices are known as microphones, and they, too, intercept sound waves and interpret them, but rather than interpret them directly into sounds as the human ear does, microphones instead translate the waves into electrical impulses or variations in electrical resistance. When these impulses are sent through a wire and into an amplifier and speaker, the electrical current is reconstituted somewhat to re-create the original pressure waves, which, when listened to by a human ear, can be interpreted as sound.

Sound comes to us from two basic sources. It is either live, occurring as it happens and as we hear it, or recorded, coming to us artificially in the form of a tape or record. Both sources of sound, which are referred to as audio, are of concern to the user of television equipment, since both sources may, at one time or another, be required.

Microphones

As stated previously, microphones are devices that electronically hear sound. However, all microphones do not hear in the same manner. They differ in terms of the system they employ to pick up the sound, such as a carbon mike, a ribbon mike, a dynamic mike, or a condenser mike. They also differ in terms of their directional sensitivity or pickup pattern.

While the human ear can discriminate sounds with considerable accuracy and quality within the human hearing range, thanks in part to our binaural hearing, microphones are not quite so sophisticated. One of the qualities that separates the human ear from the microphone is what we might call selective listening. On a daily basis, humans can and do tune in or tune out certain sounds without noticing. This is because our sense of hearing discrimination is somewhat automatic. For instance, while a person is driving, traffic noise may be high, and he may be trying to communicate with another individual through the din. His brain will attempt to suppress the random background noise in favor of the human voice. Audio enthusiasts have a gadget called an equalizer that does something similar—it allows the user selectively to emphasize or de-emphasize certain sounds. While such selective sound discrimination may not be perfect, it does, nevertheless, provide a valuable aid in aural communication.

The microphone, however, shares no such discriminatory properties. A microphone either will or will not pick up sounds. As a means to overcome this drawback, microphones have been developed that hear sounds in predetermined patterns, known as the pickup pattern. The user must determine which pickup pattern is most appropriate in terms of what he needs to do with it in obtaining quality sound for a videotape or television presentation.

Four distinct pickup patterns may be distinguished among microphones:

1. *Omnidirectional.* A microphone with an omnidirectional pickup pattern is sensitive, for the most part, to sounds coming from all directions. Such a pickup pattern tends to increase background noise and reduce the capability of focusing in upon one particular sound. Such omnidirectional microphones

are suitable for general purpose recording where no specific sound is required.
2. *Unidirectional.* Opposite of omnidirectional microphones, unidirectional microphones offer the advantage of single-point sound, that is, they will discriminate in favor of sounds at which they are aimed and suppress all other sounds. Such mikes, sometimes known as shotgun mikes, are used extensively in television and motion pictures due to their restricted pickup pattern. They provide the sound with a close-up presence without the usual echolike or background noise distraction.
3. *Cardioid.* The cardioid microphone gets its name because of its heart-shaped pickup pattern. These general purpose microphones pick up sounds from all but one direction.
4. *Bidirectional.* The bidirectional mike, a variation of the unidirectional, picks up sounds from two sides and rejects sound from the remaining two sides.

In addition to pickup patterns, microphones also come in a variety of types, including the following:

1. *Hand-held microphone.* Familiar to us from television, these small and sensitive microphones are meant to be held in the hand or on a stand while in use. Stage performers, singers, and the like use this microphone, usually with omnidirectional pickup.
2. *Boom microphone.* Intended for sound pickup where the presence of the microphone would be objectional, the boom mike is suspended on a long pole with a counterbalance at the other end. The entire pole assembly can be attached to a stationary stand or fitted to a rolling pedestal. Because of its long reach, the boom microphone can be positioned above on-camera action without intruding into the picture. Boom mikes are generally of the unidirectional or shotgun type.
3. *Lapel or lavalier microphone.* The lapel microphone has also gained in popularity thanks to its use on television. It is meant to be worn by a strap or a clip around the neck or lapel of the performer, thus freeing his hands. Such a microphone is useful in demonstrations where no

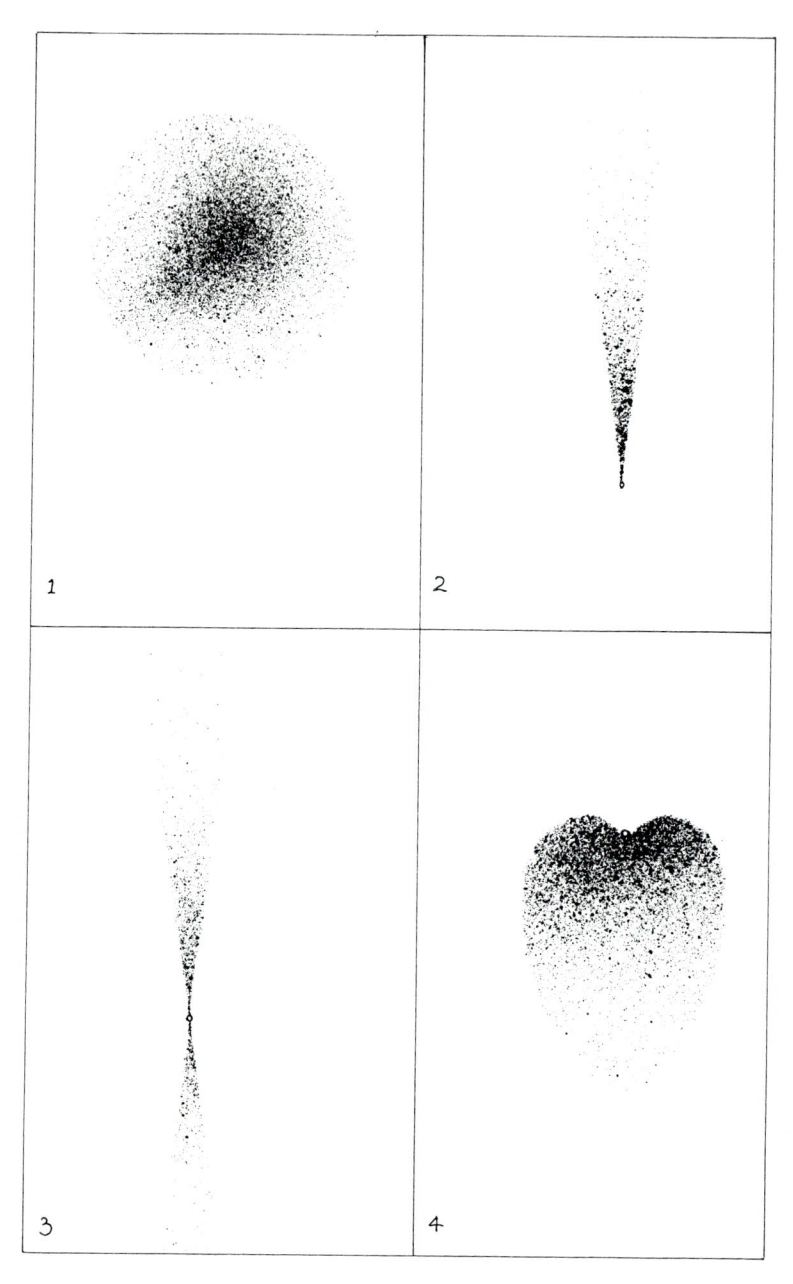

Figure 23. Common microphone pickup patterns include (1) omnidirectional, (2) unidirectional, (3) bidirectional, (4) cardioid.

boom mike is available. Such mikes are usually cardioid or omnidirectional.

Today, many microphones are built into the television camera itself. This precludes the need for hand holding the device. Such in-camera microphones are usually cardioid in pickup, although some can be of the unidirectional type.

Sometimes in a production more than one microphone (or another sound source such as recorded music or effects) may be required, such as in the case of a panel discussion. In these instances, a device known as a microphone or sound mixer allows the user to combine the sound from two or more mikes and bring the sounds together. (See Chapter 6.)

Also, there are times, when recording outdoors, that wind seriously interferes with the microphone's sound pickup. The pressure of the wind constantly activates the sound-sensitive device within the microphone, causing a continuous and distracting noise. One way to reduce such a problem is through the use of a wind screen, a soft, spongelike material that fits over the microphone and tends to break up or divert the wind so that the noise is not objectionable.

It should also be noted that some microphones require a battery for operation while others do not. Condenser microphones have excellent sound characteristics that require a battery in order to work. With such microphones the battery is placed either in the body of the mike itself or in the plug at the end of the cable.

Live sound from microphones may not, however, always be the sound required. This is particularly true in instances where the user may wish to add some background music, sound effects, or a voice that has already been recorded on audiotape. When a television production calls for audio that cannot be achieved with a live microphone, then the operator must utilize prerecorded sounds, such as are available on records and tapes. These prerecorded sounds can either be mixed with live microphone sound (through a mixer) or used directly without any microphone sounds. Whenever audio from sources other than a microphone are being used, one must be sure that the audio cable is connected to the *audio line input* receptacle of the videorecorder and not to the *mike input* receptacle.

Whether one is using a microphone or direct audio for sound, one item that must be attended to is the adjustment of the audio level. In some videorecorders, special circuitry known as AGC (automatic gain control) automatically adjusts the volume so that it is recorded at the proper level. To use this AGC mode, one merely activates the appropriate switch. One of the disadvantages of AGC is the tendency for the background noise to creep up and become louder and louder during long pauses or breaks in conversation or talking. A manual override of this function allows the user to adjust the level as he pleases.

Some units have no AGC provision at all and are strictly manual. In such situations, the unit usually contains some sort of metering device. When sound is being recorded (during a videotaping or during a sound dub), the meter should be adjusted by its control knob so that only the very loudest sounds penetrate into the plus, or red zone, of the meter. If the needle on the meter is constantly in the red zone, then the audio portion of the tape will become distorted, a condition known as overmodulation. If, on the other hand, the needle in the meter does not move enough, then the audio portion of the tape will be too low. The operator should always double-check volume levels before and during recording sessions.

Speaking before a Microphone

Speaking into a microphone is not as simple as merely talking into the air. Because of different pickup and sensitivity characteristics of microphones, and because each person speaks differently, results of a recording may not always be as they sounded when made. Three major factors affecting a microphone recording include volume level, speaker voice, and speaker distance. These three factors play an integral and interrelated role in the overall quality of microphone-recorded sound.

When the mike volume is low, the speaker must be close to the microphone. Also, the louder the speaker's voice, the lower the mike level needs to be. When low microphone levels are used, the resulting voice is purest and contains virtually no background noise. However, such mike proximity is not without its hazards.

One problem with such mike closeness is the likelihood that the mike will pick up speech idiosyncrasies, breathing, breathiness, swallowing, and so forth. Such sounds can be objectionable to the listener. Also, mike proximity increases the likelihood of overmodulating the voice. This condition, caused by excessive activation of the microphone's sound-sensing circuit, causes distortion in the recording and results in unpleasant and often unintelligible speech. One particularly severe aspect of this overmodulation, and also one of the most common problems for mike speakers, is that which occurs when pronouncing certain letters of the alphabet, such as the F, P, and T, all of which tend to pop when recorded due to the burst of air expelled from the mouth when they are pronounced. Increasing the distance between the speaker and the microphone often alleviates this problem.

When the distance between the speaker and the mike is increased, the volume on the mike must be increased. This allows much more background noise to be picked up. If the speaker is standing too far from the microphone, he creates an off-mike sound, in which case he sounds as though he is speaking to someone else instead of to the intended audience. If the speaker's voice is very weak or low, the recording runs the risk of picking up background noise, with a faint voice in the distance.

Often one may have no control over the sound situation. This is almost always the case when video operators are out in the field doing an on-the-spot taping of an event or situation. In such cases, the combination of descriptive pictures and sound should make the taped event intelligible and worthwhile.

Common sense and judgment must be used when recording with a microphone. Experience will dictate the optimum conditions that will yield a quality recording.

Chapter 9

EDITING

A Day in the Life of a Fireman, an early twentieth century short film by Edwin S. Porter, heralded the arrival of a new communication technique for the filmmaker. Working in conjunction with the Thomas A. Edison laboratories in New Jersey, Porter assembled separate filmed segments in such a way as to communicate a story. This precedent-setting achievement formed the basis of what we now know as editing.

In brief, editing is the process of arranging segments of film or videotape into a unified and meaningful presentation. Although the art of editing has attained heights of sophistication and polish, with aesthetic and philosophical overtones, in the film and television industry, its use in law enforcement television is relegated to a more rudimentary and functional role. It is the authors' concern, therefore, to present to the reader the most basic concepts of videotape editing.

There are two methods of television editing. One is through the use of a multiple-camera system in which several cameras are electronically connected to a switcher, which enables the operator to select the particular camera image that is to be fed to the videorecorder for taping. Because this form of editing necessitates not only considerable equipment but also additional personnel (more expense), which is normally beyond the reach of local police departments, it shall not be considered within the scope of this book. The second method is through the use of videorecording equipment, which allows editing with a minimum of expense.

In either case, editing principles for film and videotape are similar. Each calls for the arranging or assembling of various filmed or taped segments in accordance with a planned script or outline. This insures that the final edited production makes sense and communicates what is intended.

Editing techniques used in film and videotape are, however, quite different. Film is physically cut during editing and spliced (attached with film cement or splicing tape) into the desired sequence of the filmed presentation. With videotape, the tape itself is never actually cut. The cutting process is handled electronically, with the required segment added to or inserted at the desired point on the master tape.

To help the reader understand the basic videotape editing process, the following paragraphs will discuss the ways simple editing can be accomplished with even the most basic video equipment.

It is first necessary to examine the way a picture is recorded on a videotape. A visual inspection of motion picture film will reveal a series of frames—many individual photographic pictures—containing images that can be readily observed and understood. A visual inspection of videotape, however, will reveal nothing but a shiny magnetic coating. Yet, within this coating is the same basic frame-by-frame picture information as is contained on the film. The exception with videotape is that such information is encoded in the form of magnetic impulses invisible to the human eye but detectable to the video circuitry.

A typical recorded videotape contains three (or four) electronic information tracks. One track contains the picture information and is known as the video track. Another track (sometimes two tracks) contains sound information and is referred to as the audio track(s). The remaining track, known as a control track contains coded information that enables the signal to be properly recorded or displayed.

Because the information recorded on videotape is invisible, it is difficult, if not impossible, to match the coded frame-by-frame information correctly. If such information is not precisely aligned, the picture loses synchronization and becomes unstable and unviewable. Also, if the videotape is physically cut, not only will the picture break up at that point, but the delicate video heads may become clogged or seriously damaged. It is therefore strongly advised that videotape *always* be edited electronically.

There are three methods of videotape editing: editing with a single videorecorder, editing with two (or more) videorecorders, and convergence editing.

Editing with a Single Videorecorder

In using a single videorecorder to edit, one recorder can be used for simple editing effects using one videotape. If a videorecording is being made using a live camera or another source, such as off-the-air recording (requiring a monitor or tuner), and a sudden change in image is desired, the videorecorder can be placed in pause mode while the camera shifts to a new view. Once the camera has been satisfactorily repositioned, the pause mode can be released, and the recording can resume. The result will be a sudden change or cut from one view to another.

This method provides the most elementary and basic type of edit, known as an *assemble edit*. An assemble edit is always added to the previously taped portion. Depending upon the equipment, the cleanness of the cut will vary. With ½-inch open reel equipment, unless the operator is using a deck with a specific provision for editing (or a later model portable unit with edit pause mode), the picture will break up at the point where the tape was stopped. This breakup, known as a glitch, can range from slight tearing of the picture and loss of vertical and/or horizontal control to complete loss of picture. The glitch can last anywhere from one to six seconds.

If the operator is working with the more recent ½-inch cassette recorders, the edit point should be relatively glitch free, thanks in large part to the advanced electronic circuitry in such units.

Although the assemble edit using the single-recorder method provides results that are usable, the technique is limited and offers restricted latitude when attempting anything more ambitious. However, with the addition of another video camera and an electronic camera mixer, greater sophistication can be achieved.

Editing with Two Videorecorders

To edit with two videorecorders, two (or more) videorecorders are interconnected to permit a full range of editing possibilities, ranging from simple dubbing (duplicating a recorded videotape) to *assemble and insert* edits.

In editing, one of the videorecorders is designated as the master unit. This unit is the one that plays back the master tape. A second unit (preferably an editing deck) designated as the slave unit is responsible for recording the information in an edited form.

At this point it might be of value to mention some terminology regarding recorded videotapes. When a tape is freshly recorded directly from a live source with a camera, the tape is referred to as *first generation.* This means that the picture and sound came from the live event. When that tape is subsequently copied, or dubbed, onto another videorecorder, the copied tape is referred to as a second generation tape. If the second generation tape is then copied, or dubbed again, the third copy is referred to as a third generation tape, and so on. Each successive tape generation reduces overall picture quality. Anything beyond a second generation tape should be avoided.

Some videorecording units offer full editing capabilities, and others offer none or little. The following paragraphs will examine a simple editing situation using an open reel format editing deck and a second videorecorder (either open reel or videocassette).

The editing unit will be the slave unit, and the second deck will be the master unit. A fresh roll of blank videotape is threaded onto the slave unit. At this point, the operator should be sure to have placed the recorder in the *assemble edit mode.* The recorded tape is loaded on the master unit.

Because the recorded signal will be sent from the master unit and received by the slave unit, proper cable interconnections must be made. Also, correct cable connectors and/or adaptors must be used to interface the various recording units properly.

A cable is connected from the master unit's *video out* receptacle to the slave unit's *video in* receptacle. At this time, one should check the slave unit to be sure it is in *line mode.* If the slave unit's mode selector is in *camera mode,* no recording will be made. The connections for transfer of the picture portion of the television signal are now complete.

For the audio portion, connect a cable from the master unit's *audio out* receptacle to the slave unit's *audio line in* receptacle. If the audio cable is connected to the *mike in* receptacle, loss of sound quality will result. The connections for transfer of the audio portion of the television signal are now complete.

If the slave unit has controls for video and audio levels, these

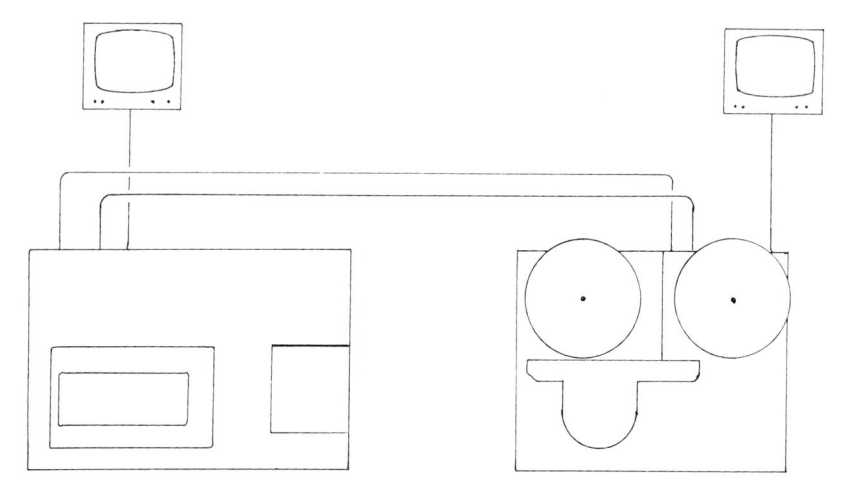

Figure 24. Videorecorder setup for editing (or dubbing) videotapes, showing the master unit (left) with video and audio out connections to monitor and to video and audio inputs of slave unit (right), which is connected to its own monitor.

should be adjusted during a test to determine the optimum recording levels. If, however, the slave unit contains an AGC (automatic gain control) circuit for video and/or audio, this will, if activated, automatically adjust video/audio levels for best picture and sound.

Each videorecorder must be connected to a television monitor/receiver in order for the editor to see what he is doing. If the recorder is of the open reel format, an 8-pin connector should be used to connect it to a monitor. If the recorder is a VCR (videocassette recorder), the RF output can be connected to the antennae terminals of a regular television receiver.

The equipment is now ready for a simple *assemble edit*. The master tape should be positioned on the master unit so that the picture is at the desired edit point. The unit is put in *pause* mode. The slave editing deck is placed at the point where the edit should begin. The tape is rewound on the slave unit to allow a six-second preroll (the user should make a note of the counter number for the edit point). The slave editing deck is started in playback mode with the editing switch set for *assemble edit*. When that point on the tape is reached, the user should release the pause mode on the master unit while depressing the edit button on the slave unit. At this point, the newly recorded material will be added at the end of the previous segment on the slave unit, resulting in an *assemble edit.*

A more sophisticated edit, known as an *insert edit,* can also be accomplished with an editing deck. An insert edit, as its name implies, is a segment of recorded material that is electronically inserted between previously recorded segments. To create an insert edit, one should follow the same procedures as for assemble edit in terms of equipment setup, being sure to switch the edit function to *insert edit mode* (for audio, video, or both).

Figure 25. An open-reel ½-inch electronic editing deck, the Sony AV-8650.

Then, the operator should locate the section of tape on the slave editing deck where new material is to be inserted. He should rewind from this point to allow for a six-second preroll. Next he should locate the section of the tape on the master unit that is to be incorporated into the edited tape and place the master unit in *pause mode.* He then starts playback on the slave unit until the desired edit point is reached. Then, the operator should release the pause mode on the master unit while depressing the edit button. When the transferred segment is complete, he should depress the edit release button on the slave unit. The edit is now complete.

There is more to editing, however, than the mere technical joining of segments. In fact, in the film industry, the individual responsible for joining film is known as a film cutter, and he is considered a highly specialized technician. The film cutter scrupulously follows the film editor's instructions on how to cut the film; however, he plays a minor role, if any at all, in deciding which segments to use and where to place them. That is the job of the editor himself.

Where a segment is placed and how long that segment runs is of critical importance in creating a unifying continuity and meaningfulness to the television production. It is this critical judgment that makes the editor's role significant. The editor in a television production facility such as is the concern of this book must not only master the technique of editing but also the art of editing.

Convergence Editing

In convergence editing an electronic editing device is interfaced between two compatible videocassette recorders (convergence editing as discussed here will not work with open reel ½-inch equipment). The master (or blank) tape is placed in one recorder, and the slave (or prerecorded) tape is placed in the other recorder. Edit points are selected by depressing the edit button on the convergence editor at the desired point for both the master and slave unit. The convergence editor will then automatically rewind the tapes so that the edit points will converge at the correct location. All edits are completed automatically with relative ease.

One important concept to keep in mind during editing is something called *stream of consciousness*. This is a basic film concept (also applicable to videotape) that deals with the phenomenon of understanding a film (or videotape) merely by being exposed to one related picture or scene after another. The sequence and logic of the related pictures are strung together within the brain where they become meaningful and make sense.

Whether the tape is purely technical or artistic, the various images it uses and the manner in which they are edited is crucial to how the viewer will interpret and understand that tape.

Chapter 10

TITLING

Whatever videotape production is planned, whether it is a drunk driver test or a public relations promotion, the video production will need some sort of title either for embellishment or for program identification. Titling can be as simple or as complex as one wishes to make it. There are, however, four relatively simple methods of putting titles into a videotape production to give it a professional and official touch.

Titling by Typewriter

Surprisingly enough, a regular typewriter can be put to use to create reasonable titles with very little fuss or bother. Although a typewriter with pica type yields letter impressions that are slightly larger than elite, and therefore more desirable, either style will work satisfactorily. One should make sure the typewriter chosen has letters that are clean and make good impressions. If necessary, the letters may be scrubbed with a toothbrush or oil-based modeling clay may be pressed against each letter head to pull out the ink residue.

If possible, a film (sometimes known as carbon) ribbon should replace the standard fiber ribbon common to most typewriters. Film ribbons yield extremely black impressions. A new fiber ribbon, however, will do.

Next the video operator should decide on the titles he wishes to have on the videotape. It is best to avoid cluttering a single frame with too many letters. If necessary, more than one title card should be prepared, and each should appear in sequence. This makes reading the titles easier.

The approximate aspect ratio of the television screen should be considered when typing the titles. It is helpful to think in terms of four units horizontally by three units vertically. The letters should not come close to either limit; one should use more than a single line of type if this is necessary. Also, using all caps rather than caps and lowercase letters will make the titles easier to read.

If color is desired on the titles, they can be typed on colored paper, but the color selected must not make the letters difficult to read. Deep blue paper with black type, for example, will be difficult to read on the television screen.

Titling with Transfer Type

Transfer type is an ingenious method of achieving professional-quality lettering without too much fuss. Used by commercial artists in advertising for many years, this product, available at art stores in sheets, contains an enormous variety of lettering styles, colors, and sizes. All that is necessary is to select the size, style, and color transfer sheet. If the titles are short, such as one or two words, or perhaps the date, then a light horizontal line across a clean sheet of paper can be used as a guide in aligning each letter. If centering is critical, then the person making the titles will have to count the number of characters and spaces in each line of the titles, dividing the total by two and counting across the title until he reaches that number. The character or space appearing there is the center of the title. By measuring the paper upon which the letters are to be transfered to find its center point, and by starting the letter transfer from the center point and working out to the left and to the right, one can be assured of centered titles.

To transfer letters, the person merely places the appropriate letter on the transfer sheet over the area on the paper where it is to appear. Gently rubbing on the back side of the transfer sheet over the letter using a soft pencil or a ball-point pen and lifting the transfer sheet will transfer the letter to the paper below. If the transfer does not work, one should try again. It may be possible that the sheet of paper contains some grease or other foreign materials, or the transfer sheet may be very old or dried out. If the transfer does not work, it should be thrown away and a new, fresh sheet purchased.

When the lettering has been completed, the letters should be rubbed down more permanently using the burnishing sheet supplied with the transfer sheet. It is simply placed over the word or title and rubbed gently, with all letters covered. The burnishing sheet is then removed, and the titles are finished. The result is clean, neat, and professional-looking lettering. With a little practice, quality lettering effects can be produced quickly and easily.

Titling with Stencils

A variety of styles and sizes of letter stencil sheets is available. For this method, the person lightly draws a line across the paper where he wishes the titles to appear. Each stencil letter is placed one at a time on the line and drawn in with a dark pencil. When the word or title is complete, the letters may be colored in so they appear solid, or their outline may be darkened. Such titles are now ready for use.

Removable Rub Ons

Removable rub ons are similar to transfer type, with the exception that these letters are much more resilient to use and can be removed and reused. Rub ons offer a quick and clean method of creating titles. It is important to select a color that will contrast sufficiently with the background. One then proceeds as with transfer letters, one letter at a time.

The overall quality and appearance of titling will have an impact upon the quality of the production. Common sense will dictate when elaborate titles may be required and when simple, typed titles will suffice.

Chapter 11

PROGRAM FORMATS AND SCRIPTING

Almost everything in video will by necessity require some sort of plan of action to insure that things flow smoothly. Such a plan of action takes into consideration the program format and results in a script.

There are six basic program formats, plus many variations that can be utilized to build a program. Each format will generate its own type of script.

1. *The lecture.* The straightforward lecture format calls for the on-camera person to talk to the camera as an instructor talks to a class. This approach is useful for information dissemination and/or demonstration purposes; however, such a format runs the risk of becoming tiresome and boring unless it is enhanced with visual inserts such as illustrations, recorded video segments, film, photographs, graphs, charts, documents, maps, and so forth. The lecture format, when fully utilized to take advantage of the tremendous possibilities of video, can be an effective teaching tool.
2. *The discussion.* The discussion is a familiar format that allows a number of panelists to discuss topics of importance, relevance, and interest, usually with one person serving as moderator. The discussion format allows the presentation of numerous points of view on a particular topic.
3. *The debate.* A debate presents two (or more) sides to an important issue using adversary positions. Such a format can be made more interesting with the inclusion of visuals such as photos, film, charts, maps, and the like.
4. *The dramatic presentation.* In a dramatic presentation, performers assume various roles to emphasize or dramatize events for instructional or entertainment purposes.

5. *The documentary.* The documentary usually studies in-depth a particular subject or event and requires considerable advance research and planning. Many visual materials, such as photographs, illustrations, films, and videotapes are essential in making a documentary not only successful but interesting.
6. *The interview.* In the interview, one individual is questioned by one or more interviewers.

Each of the program formats mentioned requires some sort of outline or guide to follow. This outline or guide is known as a script, and contrary to common belief, a script does not necessarily have to be a word-by-word account of what is to be said. A script can come in a variety of types.

1. *The full script.* The full script is one in which every word to be spoken, every camera angle and shot to be taken, and every sound to be heard is precisely timed, cued, and indicated in writing. While the on-camera performers execute the script, the behind-the-scenes staff, from the director to the crew, carefully follows the full script step by step, direction by direction, word by word. This insures that the result will be as close as possible to the initial program concept. A full script is generally required for dramatic presentation program formats.
2. *The semiscript.* In the semiscript type, the spoken parts are indicated or suggested in general but not written out in detail, word for word. Camera movement and sound effects are also indicated, with their success dependent upon the experience and common sense of the director, camera, and sound operators.
3. *The format script.* The format script is an outline that lists in order of performance each act or sequence to be taped. Accompanying this is a running time for the entire program and for each segment.
4. *Fact sheet (rundown sheet).* A fact sheet merely lists those objects and people which will appear on camera along with a very rough indication of what is to be said. This script type relies heavily upon ad-lib (in which the on-camera person speaks extemporaneously but relevantly to the topic and

within broad topic parameters with nothing but his intellect and common sense to guide what he says and does).

The typical script has a particular format to it dictated by the needs of television production. The format includes provision for audio (sound) and video (picture) instructions. Usually the right half of the script page is dedicated to audio instructions (including cueing of music, mike on and off, and so on) as well as dialogue, and the left half is dedicated to the video portion (which camera, what lens, whether to fade in and out, whether to superimpose images and titles, and so forth). To avoid confusion, it is desirable to type all audio and video instructions *in upper-case letters only*, but all dialogue is typed in upper- and lower-case letters.

Some scripts may include a column for effects, camera selection or camera angle or type of shot, timings, and the like; however, on small productions, such items can usually be indicated in handwritten notation directly on the script.

When a large production is undertaken, an updated script should be handed to each person connected with the taping with their responsibilities marked on the script by the director.

The importance of a script to any production cannot be overestimated. The script serves as a guide and outline to insure that a smooth and uniform production results.

Following are examples of the full script and the semiscript.

Full Script

Production date:

Video	*Audio*
CAM-1 slide of headquarters	MUSIC: "Swat Theme" 35 sec.
CAM-2 CU host	ANN.: Welcome to "Crime Prevention in your Community." Today's topic will cover making your home burglar resistant. During the next few minutes, we will be presenting the various types of locks that are available for the home.
CAM-1 CU lock 1	ANN.: Here you see one of the more

	common locks known as a double dead bolt. This lock is used primarily where there is glass alongside a doorway, which an individual could break, reach in, and open the lock.
	The double dead bolt requires a key to open the door from inside the home and prevents a person from easily opening the lock.
CAM-2 MS HOST	ANN.: Selection of the lock depends largely on its use. For example, the next lock is used to secure a sliding glass door.
CAM-1 CU–LOCK 2	ANN.: As you can see, this lock is sturdier than the usual sliding glass door lock. It provides extra security and protection.
CAM-1 MED. HOST	ANN.: And now, let's examine locks useful in commercial business enterprises.

Semiscript

Production date:

Video	*Audio*
C-2 slide of police headquarters	MUSIC: "Swat Theme" 35 sec.
C-1 CU HOST	ANN.: Welcome and opening remarks.
C-2 CU–LOCK 1	ANN.: Intro to lock.
C-1 MS–HOST	ANN.: Speaks about lock selection.
C-2 CU–LOCK 2	ANN.: ... sliding glass lock ...
C-1 MED–HOST	ANN.: commercial business locks

Note: In the preceding examples, abbreviations have been used for camera directions. These plus other standardized terms include the following:

ANN—announcer
CU—close-up

ECU — extreme close-up
MS — medium shot
PAN — turn camera left and/or right
TILT — aim camera up or down

Part Two
APPLYING TELEVISION

Chapter 12

TRAINING THE OPERATOR

One of the most crucial and integral aspects of the entire videotape program is the training of the videotape operators. No matter how much equipment is owned by the police department, it is totally useless unless the equipment can be *properly* used.

A properly trained operator is necessary because of the relative ease with which an untrained person can damage the video equipment. The courts also require that a video operator be trained in the use of the equipment in order to allow his videotape to be entered into evidence. It is not necessary for videotape operators to have knowledge of the electronic principles behind the equipment. Court decisions have stated that operators who give breath analysis tests do not have to know how the equipment works, but they must have knowledge of how to set up and properly use the equipment. The same holds true for videotape. The operators *must* be able to show that they are able to set up and properly operate the television equipment.

Many police academies are offering courses in video operation. These courses should be taught by individuals with police experience and not by nonpolice personnel who only have television experience. The instructor who is both a police officer and a trained video instructor is able to present the students with both videotaping knowledge and its proper and correct applications for law enforcement. A person with no police experience may be able to teach *how* to tape a drunk driver, but unless he has been involved in a drunk driver arrest, he may be unfamiliar with the law and normal police procedure and may present faulty information.

Even though many academies are offering these courses, the police department may still have to provide instruction to officers if it is unable to send men to the academy or if it wishes to present additional instruction. The following chapters will give the course instructor the basic information he requires to train the students.

It is imperative that the department select its instructor carefully. He must be both an excellent police officer and a capable instructor. It is particularly helpful if the instructor has had some form of methods of instruction course and is familiar with correct teaching techniques. This course *cannot* be taught by the lecture method of instruction alone. If the instructor is not the person who will set up or be responsible for the overall videotape program, he must work hand in hand with the overseer so that instruction and implementation flow smoothly.

The first thing that the police instructor should do is to familiarize himself with his department's equipment. Many manufacturers or dealers will provide a training course for instructors when their brand of video equipment is purchased. This course should enable the instructor to teach a basic videotape course.

The instructor must also meet with the magistrate for the court in which the video evidence will be presented. The magistrate may have certain requirements that must be adhered to either in training or in program development. Many magistrates require that video operators have a minimum number of hours in training before they may be certified as operators. If this is the case, the instructor must develop his lesson plans accordingly. The magistrate may also require, for example, that the breath test be videotaped when being administered to a drunk driver. The instructor must incorporate any judicial requirements into his course of instruction.

Judicial approval of the instructor's training credentials should be obtained from the magistrate. This will enable the instructor to conduct his training class with the approval of the court. The instructor should develop a lesson plan that will be followed when conducting training. This ensures that each student will be presented with the same material and also ensures that nothing will be overlooked in the training process.

The lesson plan should contain lesson objectives (what the instructor wishes to accomplish during instruction) and performance objectives (what the student will be able to perform after the training) along with his plan for instruction. A sample lesson plan may appear as follows:

> *Lesson Objective:* To present the student with information on the various formats available in video.
> *Performance Objective:* The student will be able to list the major formats in videotape and be able to describe the differences in formats.
> *Instructor's Notes:* Discuss the various formats. Cover 1-inch recorders, ¾-inch recorders, ½-inch reel-to-reel recorders, ½-inch VHS recorders, ½-inch Beta recorders, and ¼-inch recorders. Explain the various uses of the recorders, difficulties in using the large format recorders, tape differences, loading differences, and pros and cons of using each type of recorder or format.

METHOD OF INSTRUCTION: DISCUSSION, LECTURE, DEMONSTRATION.

The lesson plan will cover each area of material that the instructor will present and will enable the instructor to develop tests based on the material presented. (For further information on developing lesson plans, see *How To Teach Police Subjects: Theory and Practice* by Leonard Harrison, published by Charles C Thomas, Publisher, Springfield, Illinois.) The instructor will also note various types of visual aids that may be used in his teaching. For example, he may show the various types of formats to the students by use of photographs and slides, or he may show the actual recorders.

After the lesson plan is properly developed, the instructor is ready to begin his training program. If the individual who is selected to teach the course is able to attend a methods of instruction (MOI) course at either the police academy or at the college level, it will make his job much easier. The MOI course will prepare the new teacher in most aspects of instructing. This course will present information that will be useful not only for the teaching of the television class but for any course that is to be presented. Once the basic teaching skills are learned, they can be adapted to almost any area of instruction.

In the MOI class, the new instructor will be given information on the development of course objectives, performance objectives, and lesson plans. He will be shown the use of various audiovisual aids along with the appropriate times to utilize them in his presentation. He will also be critiqued on various presentations that he will have to prepare and then deliver before his classmates. This is the time for him to correct his teaching deficiencies and to develop his strong points. The MOI course is helpful to both the seasoned instructor and the novice, since the experienced instructor may be able to refine his teaching skills.

After the instructor has finished his lesson plan, he can then begin his training program. Some important subjects to cover are as follows:

1. *Videotape.* An explanation of the various formats of videotape recording should be given. The student should be familiar with the various types of equipment and formats because a defense attorney may question the operator in court concerning this area of videotaping. The operator needs information on the basic format types and their differences for his courtroom testimony. The instructor should also develop a packet of handouts for the students. These handouts should contain all forms that are used during the taping process. Handouts on the various connectors used in videotape, editing techniques, wiring instructions for equipment setup, along with information on the department's equipment, can be developed. The student should also be given his copy of the drunk driver checklist, which is developed by the instructor. This is a step-by-step guideline for the drunk driving taping from beginning to end. (A sample checklist is presented in Chapter 13.)

2. *Equipment setup and operation.* The instructor should stress the correct manner of equipment handling and techniques for a good production. Setting up and handling the equipment the department owns should be demonstrated and explained. The manufacturer, model, and format should be presented during this phase of training. This information is frequently asked in court, and the operator must know the type of equipment he is using. The student must also know the maximum taping time of the recorder using various lengths of videotape.

3. *Taping the drunk driver.* Since the main use of video equipment today is in the use of drunk driving taping, the instructor should

concentrate most of his efforts on how to tape the drunken driver properly. Chapter 13 of this book covers taping of the drunk driver, and it should be read thoroughly before training. The training should be conducted in the room where the videotaping will take place. If it is impractical to conduct the training in this room, a mock setup should be constructed for the students to practice taping. All aspects of taping should be demonstrated. The student should be able, at the completion of training, to set up all necessary equipment and be able to follow the drunk driver checklist. Any deviation from department policy or the drunk driver checklist cannot be allowed. If a problem is discovered during training, the student should be made immediately aware of the problem so that incorrect habits are not developed.

4. *Hands-on instruction.* The course must include a large amount of hands-on equipment operation. Each student must demonstrate to the instructor his ability to set up, operate, and take down the equipment. The instructor should stress during this training the various techniques that are desirable when taping the drunk driver. Each operator should be shown when to zoom in on the drunk to emphasize his condition. For example, when the finger-to-nose test is being taped, the operator should zoom in close to show where the drunk is touching his nose. The operator also should lock the camera in position on the tripod when he is taping any test that is meant to show the subject swaying. If the camera is not locked in position, the defense attorney may be able to say that the supposed swaying of his client is in reality caused by the movements of the cameraman.

If the instructor wishes to demonstrate incorrect techniques in order for the students to recognize the problems of taping, he *must* show the correct techniques immediately following. If an incorrect procedure is shown without correction, it is conceivable that the student may only remember the incorrect demonstration.

5. *Various uses of videotape.* The various uses of videotaping should be covered, such as its use in taping confessions, surveillance taping, training tapes, traffic surveys, public relations, and major crime scenes.

Classroom demonstrations and field exercises should be included to enable the student to demonstrate to the instructor his knowledge in each area. Mock setups of crime scenes and confessions help make the training realistic and meaningful. It is very difficult to determine whether or not a student has understanding of a particular technique unless he has had a chance to demonstrate his mastery. The classes should be taken on a tour of a cable TV or college television station to give them insight into major production aspects. It is expected that this tour will provide the students with a major resource for taping assistance and editing in departmental productions. It is very useful to have a studio available for use in taping public relations and crime prevention programming.

6. *Mock courtroom.* It is advisable for the instructor to conduct a mock courtroom setup at the completion of the course in which the student is asked to qualify himself as a video operator for the court. The instructor will be the judge in this court with students acting as prosecutor, defense attorney, defendant, and arresting officer.

Each student is required to videotape another student, who is to play the role of the drunk driver. The video operator will conduct himself as if it were an actual case and prepare all necessary paperwork and documents for court. He will present the case to his prosecutor, who will then present the case to the court. The defense attorney and defendant will be given discovery on the case and will attempt to defend it before the court.

The instructor will decide on the case, paying particular attention to the presentation and testimony of the video operator. He will view the tape for correct procedures and decide on the merits of the case based on the drunk's actions on tape along with the testimony of the arresting officer. This will give the participants a feeling for what they will face in court. All students in the class should be required to play each role at least one time.

In order to facilitate the presentation, the judge should have questions prepared that must be asked of each player. For example, the prosecutor should ask the videotape operator questions as to his qualifications for operating the equipment, the type of equipment used, and the procedures for safeguarding the taped evidence.

The defense attorney should attempt to disqualify the operator and attempt to have the tape barred from admission as evidence.

The instructor should have the assistance of his municipal judge or prosecutor to develop the questions for the mock courtroom. The instructor will, of course, modify the course to meet his department's particular needs. The number of hours of training will depend on a number of factors. The length will depend on the extent of material presented, the number of students in the class (more students in the class means more time, since each student will have to be provided with hands-on training), and, of course, the number of hours required by the magistrate. One magistrate may require only five hours of training while another may require twenty.

At the completion of training, the instructor should issue a certificate or card to the trained operator. Once the instructor has received judicial approval of his training course, these certificates will help prevent the instructor from having to testify in court. The card is similar to those issued for the breath analysis machines. It should state that "Officer _____ of the Hometown Police Department has successfully completed a course of instruction in the proper operation and use of videotape recording equipment." The card should contain the date of completion and the signature of the instructor.

Many smaller departments will find that this type of training setup is too cumbersome for their needs. If an instructor has a student on a one-to-one basis, his training can be more personal. He should still have his lesson plan developed so that the training is basically the same for each student. If, however, the student will be permanently assigned to drunk driving taping and will not be conducting videotaped surveillances, he can adjust his training to the needs of the department. He will certify this student as being certified in the use of videotape for drunk driving taping. This student would not be allowed to conduct a taped surveillance until trained to do so by the instructor. The completion of the basic training course does not signal the end of the operator's training but the beginning. The operator should be requalified with the equipment periodically and should be brought up to date with any changes in taping procedure or equipment usage.

Each department should purchase books on videotaping, which should be required reading for each operator. The student need not be tested on his reading of the material, but the instructor should give the students ample time while on duty to digest the material.

The instructor should also review his training material before each course begins. Rapid changes in technology may change some areas of the presentation to the student. Any changes in content should be made and incorporated into the lesson plans. He should also follow the progress of his students after the completion of training. He should review their finished tapes and, if necessary, provide the student with *constructive criticism* on his mistakes. Courtroom testimony of the operators should be checked to ensure that there are no major problems in the courtroom. The students should be encouraged to ask questions of the instructor even after training. This will give the instructor feedback as to any problems that the students may be having.

It is imperative that the instructor keep a list of certified students along with their date of certification. He should also keep a photocopy of any certificate that is issued to the operator. This will assist in the discovery process should a particular tape be needed for a not guilty plea.

The key to the entire videotaping program is the trained operator. Without him, the video equipment would be given the distinction of sitting in the closet since no one would know how or why to use it. It is hoped that the trained operators will be instrumental in having neglected equipment come out of the closet and being put to use.

Chapter 13

TAPING THE DRUNK DRIVER

The drunk driver has become one of the leading causes of automobile accidents throughout the United States. Many of the states that had lowered their drinking ages have raised them to their previous age requirements. It was statistically proven that when the drinking age was lowered to the age of eighteen, the number of automobile accidents involving the eighteen to twenty-one age group dramatically increased.

As an example, in 1981 in New Jersey, the drinking age was eighteen. For this year there were 47,924 accidents involving people aged eighteen to twenty. Of these, there were 18,523 accidents involving injuries and 202 fatal accidents. There were 59 drunken driving arrests (27.4%). For the year 1982 (in which the drinking age was raised to nineteen), there were 46,666 accidents involving eighteen-, nineteen-, and twenty-year-old drivers. Of these there were 17,717 injuries and 175 fatal accidents. There were 57 drunken driving arrests (31.3%). These statistics show that once the drinking age was raised just one year, to nineteen, the number of accidents decreased, as did the number of injuries and fatalities. The percentage of drunken driving arrests was increased; however, the actual number of drunken drivers (59 in 1981 and 57 in 1982) was decreased. Statistics including all age groups for the first six months of 1983 show that there were 386 fatal accidents and 402 persons killed. This is 34 fewer fatal accidents and 60 fewer deaths compared with the same period in 1982. In 1981 there were 1,043 fatal accidents, and 1,162 people were killed. In 1982, fatal accidents dropped to 985, with 1,061 people killed. In 1981, alcohol was a factor in 57.8 percent of the fatalities but dropped to 55.4 percent in 1982.

During 1981, there were 5,529 drunken driving arrests for persons under twenty-one years of age, and 7,086 in 1982. The first quarter of 1983 produced 1,446 drunken driving arrests in the age group under twenty-one years old. In the first four months of 1983, there were 9 fatalities in this age group under the influence of alcohol. In the first four months of 1982, there were 21 alcohol-related deaths in this age group. Total figures are not yet available for 1983, in which the age was raised to twenty-one. There should be statistically fewer accidents for this age group once the figures are released.

It was also learned that eighteen-year-olds were purchasing alcoholic beverages and frequently distributing them to those under eighteen. This was found to be due to the fact that the eighteen-year-old was still in high school and in contact with younger students.

In New Jersey, the drinking age had been lowered from twenty-one to eighteen years in 1973. In 1982, the age was raised to nineteen. In 1983, just ten years from the date the drinking age was lowered, the age was once again raised to twenty-one years. The law did contain a grandfather clause that enabled those who were nineteen before the law was passed to retain their right to drink.

The drinking of alcoholic beverages has long been ingrained in the American way of life, as is the use of the automobile. It is when the two are mixed that the police officer becomes concerned.

The drinking driver has become a problem of immense magnitude. Police administrators have justifiably intensified their enforcement efforts in attempting to reduce the instances of drinking and driving. Federal and state grants have provided the monetary backing to help fund the efforts of the local departments. Funds have been provided for both manpower and equipment. Audiovisual grants have seeded the programs for the videotaping of the drunk driver, and videotaping the drunk driver has proven to be an effective tool of evidence for the prosecution of the drunk driver.

Since many states have increased the penalities for drunken driving, the instances of not guilty pleas for the offense have risen dramatically, however. Videotaping the drunken driver while he is performing coordination tests can help to increase the department's conviction rate.

The Wyckoff, New Jersey, Police Department began taping drunken drivers in May of 1981. Since the start of the program, over 100 drunken driving arrests have been videotaped. A conviction rate of approximately 98 percent has been achieved when videotape evidence has been presented (these statistics are the norm for departments that have started a comprehensive drunken driving program). The majority of defendants entered a guilty plea after the defense attorney viewed the tape. Even when a not guilty plea has been entered, the defendant is normally found guilty after the case is presented in court.

It is imperative that the department plan a program for the videotaping of the drunken driver and establish guidelines and procedures for the use of the equipment. The program should be thoroughly planned before any equipment is purchased. One or two individuals should be selected to design the program and to report their progress to their superior officer.

Several important steps should be taken prior to implementation of any program:

1. *A meeting should be held with the magistrate of the court in which the videotaped evidence will be presented.* The judge should be consulted about any specific requirements or guidelines that he may require for the evidence to be admissible in court.

Most magistrates will require at the minimum that a clock and calendar be visible in the tape at all times during the testing of the drunken driver. It is generally required that once the taping has begun the tape not be stopped for *any* reason. (This will be fully discussed later in the chapter.)

Some magistrates have required that the defendant sign his name on a blackboard or flip chart when the taping has begun.

The majority of departments will tape all coordination testing of the defendant along with questioning about specific areas concerning the arrest.

The taping of the breath analysis test varies from locality to locality, depending on the wishes of each magistrate. The Wyckoff Police Department does *not* tape the breath testing. This has not detrimentally affected the department's clearance rate.

The magistrate must also present his requirements for the training of the videotape operator. No judicial guidelines have been

Figure 26. Clock, calendar, and department name are shown on camera while an officer reads the video operator's form prior to a drunk driver taping.

established nationwide to set a minimum amount of training required. The training varies from a low of two hours to a high of sixty hours. As long as the magistrate is satisfied as to the operator's training, then the tape can be admitted.

Since the operator need only testify that he has knowledge of the operation of the equipment and that it accurately recorded what took place, the magistrate many times will depend on the training officer's recommendation as to the hours of training necessary. The magistrate can take judicial notice of the training if a certificate is presented to the certified operator. The certificate must be signed by the training officer, and his credentials should be established for the court. (The subject of training is fully covered in Chapter 12 of this book.)

2. *Standard forms should be developed for use in the drunk driving program.* The forms should be reviewed by the department's legal officer and the magistrate. One form is prepared for reading on camera by the videotape operator/cameraman. Another form is to be read by the arresting officer, again on camera. The forms should be mimeographed so that no deviation from the text is permitted.

Samples of these forms are presented in Appendices D and E at the back of this book and will serve as guidelines for preparation. The camera operator's form should contain *at the minimum* the name and badge number of the operator along with the name of the department. The correct date and time should also be presented. The name of the defendant and his address, along with the name of the arresting officer and time of the arrest, should be included. A statement that the testing is being video recorded and that the person was arrested for driving under the inluence of alcohol is a necessity. This precludes the defendant's claiming that he had no knowledge that he was being videotaped.

The form should also include space to record the starting and ending numbers on the tape counter of the recorder along with the total taping time of the testing. The form must be signed by the videotape operator.

The arresting officer's form will contain a statement that the defendant has been arrested for a violation of the drunk driving law and that a videotape recording is being made of all of his actions. He will also be informed that he and his attorney will be permitted to view the tape before his trial.

3. *A third form, the chain of evidence waiver form, is necessary for the viewing of any videotape.* This form is important to preserve the chain of evidence for the videotape. Since the normal chain of

Figure 27. Officer is shown reading the arresting officer's form on camera, with monitor displaying videorecorded image.

evidence requirement is applicable to the tape, the department must take appropriate steps for its preservation. This form should be mimeographed and contain at the minimum the case number, name of the defendant, his address, and his date of arrest. It should contain a statement attesting that the tape was viewed by the defendant or his defense attorney and the date of viewing. The person viewing the tape *must* sign the form attesting to this fact.

If the videotape operator is not available to view the tape, the tape can be shown by another qualified videotape operator, *providing that the defense attorney or his defendant waives the chain of evidence in writing.* The viewing form should include a section for the waiving of the chain of evidence that will include a line for the attorney's/ defendant's signature. The tape should not be shown by another officer unless this waiver is agreed to. The majority of magistrates will allow the tape to be admitted into evidence without the second officer having to appear in court. A sample of this form is also presented in an appendix of this book (see Appendix F).

4. *A log book must be maintained to provide immediate access and referral for pertinent information on each videotaped session.* Each videotape and sleeve, when purchased, should be numbered consecutively for identification.

The log book should contain information concerning the date of the taping, the name and address of the person arrested, the names of the arresting officer and videotape operator, case number, evidence locker number (all tapes must be placed in an evidence locker after the session), tape number, disposition of the case, and the date that the tape was erased along with the name of the officer who erased the tape. This log book must be completed by each videotape operator immediately after taping has been finished.

5. *A room should be selected and appropriately arranged for the taping sessions.* The room should be selected that will prevent the taping from being interrupted. A room with a door should be selected so that personnel will not enter when taping is in progress. It should be sufficiently soundproofed so that random noises from outside of the room will not be heard.

The room should be spacious enough to allow all coordination testing to be performed. There should be enough room to allow proper camera movement to record all events. A black or white stripe (to contrast with the floor coloring) should be placed on the floor, perpendicular to the camera. This line will serve as the line when the defendant walks the line.

The wall coloring should be neutral, one that will be suitable for taping. A neutral gray or pale yellow will suffice.

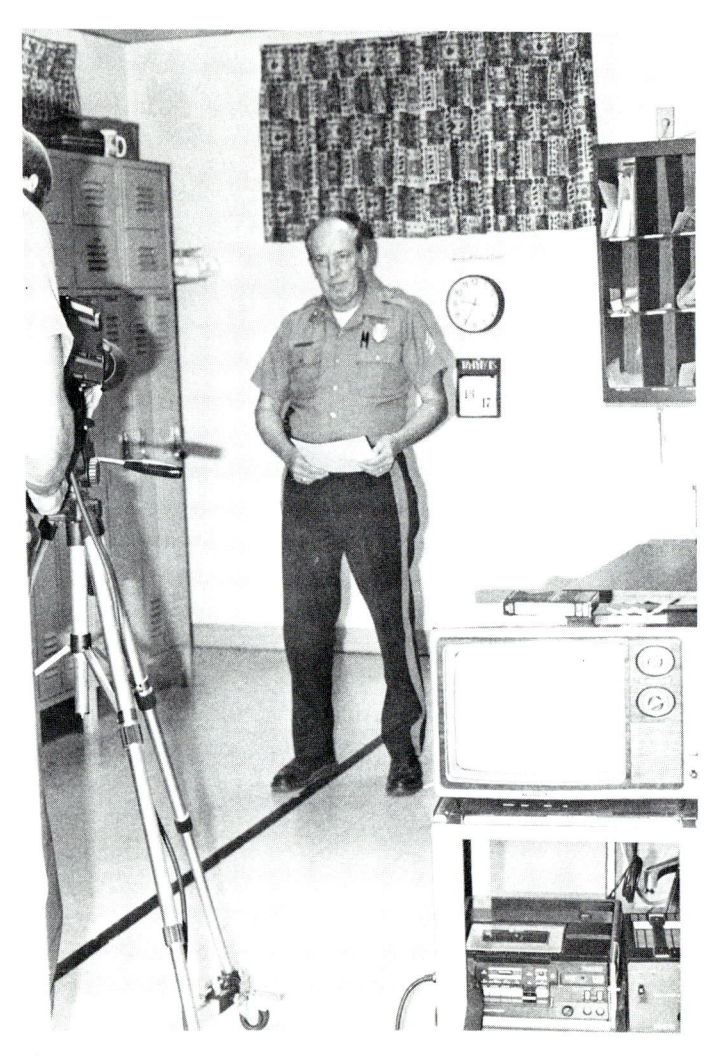

Figure 28. Relationship of on-camera officer to camera and operator.

A clock and calendar should be positioned on the wall opposite the camera location. These items should be in the camera viewfinder as much as possible to eliminate any question about the tape being stopped and restarted. The department's name and or emblem should also be on the wall to identify the taping agency.

All auxiliary lighting, if required, should be permanently fixed. This will eliminate setting up lights with each taping session. It must be remembered that one should *never* aim the lights into the face of the suspect. If lights are in his eyes, he can claim that his test performance was affected by the lighting. This may hurt the case in court.

Microphones should also be permanently wired in place. The location that affords the best sound recording should be selected. Once the microphone is permanently in place, it can be plugged into the recorder when needed.

The floor of the room must be kept free of wires and obstacles. Any irregularity in the floor will cause the camera to move when dollied (moving the camera position either in or out).

Once the initial preparation has been made and the equipment has been purchased, it can be put into service. The equipment should be stored in the same room where the taping is being conducted.

The camera should be stored on the tripod and covered with a plastic bag for protection. The recorder, power supply, and monitor/television set should be placed on a wheeled cart. The television is placed on the upper portion of the cart, and the recorder/power supply is placed on the bottom shelf. A power strip should be affixed to the cart for plugging in the units. This cart will allow compact storage and easy movement of the equipment.

All blank videotapes should be numbered consecutively on both the tape and the tape sleeve. This will enable ready identification of the tape and will prevent a tape from being placed in the incorrect sleeve. A simple label maker is sufficient for this task.

A checklist should be printed for each operator to refresh his memory before and during taping. A sample checklist is as follows:

1. Ensure that the time is correct on the clock and that the date is correct on the calendar.
2. Set up the videorecorder and camera and check the cable connectors for proper hookup. Connect power supply to the alternating current. Position recorder and camera in proper location.

Figure 29. Equipment should be stored in the same room where the taping is conducted.

3. Turn on auxiliary lighting and connect auxiliary microphone. Ensure that the television set is on the correct channel for use with the videorecorder. Most sets will have to be on channel 3 or channel 4. The correct channel will depend on the area of the country, since a blank channel is used for the playback.
4. Complete the forms for the videotape operator and the arresting officer. These are to be read on camera. The videotape operator reads his form, which is followed by the arresting officer reading his form. The defendant is on camera during the reading of the forms.
5. Place a *fresh unrecorded* or *completely erased* videocassette tape into the recorder.
6. Set the tape counter on the videorecorder to 000.
7. The videotape operator will then conduct a test tape to ensure that the recording system is functioning properly. It is possible to have an image on the television set before the tape is rolling and not have the image recorded on the tape. It is therefore imperative that a test be conducted with the equipment. This test will consist of both a video and audio check. In order to conduct the test, the video operator will start the tape rolling and walk on camera. He will speak in a normal voice in a count from one to ten. He will then stop the recorder and play back the test tape. If the recording is satisfactory, he will commence taping. If there is a problem with the audio or video, he will attempt to correct the problem. If he is unsuccessful, he will not conduct the taping and will refer the problem to the proper individual. After the playback of the test tape, the tape will be rewound to the beginning, and the taping can be started. The test tape will automatically be erased as the taping of the defendant is conducted.
8. The tape of the coordination test should be started by fading into the scene. This is accomplished by turning the lens opening on the camera (while the tape is rolling) from the c (closed) position and slowly opening the camera lens until the best picture is observed in the viewfinder. If an auto-iris lens is used, the lens will be moved from the c

(closed) position to the a (auto) position, and the camera will automatically adjust for the room light.

This fade-in will help to eliminate any picture instability that results from the tape starting up from a complete stop. *Make sure that the tape is visually inspected at this point to ensure that the tape is moving.* Many times a cameraman will think that a scene is being recorded and later discover that the tape never started rolling. *It is important to remember that it is possible to have a picture in the camera viewfinder and on the monitor but not have the tape rolling.*

9. The first scene on camera should be of the defendant standing alongside the clock and calendar. The videotape operator will then walk on camera and deliver his statement, which is printed on the videotape operator's form. He will then return to the camera and will tape the arresting officer delivering his statement. *Once the taping has begun, the recorder is not stopped for any reason until the taping is completed.* Anytime that the tape is stopped, it allows a defense attorney to question the validity of the taping, since there will be a question as to what transpired while the tape was shut down. The only reason for a tape to be stopped is because of equipment malfunction or power stoppage. Even this will have to be satisfactorily explained in court. It is very easy to tell whether a tape is stopped and restarted, since a picture disruption, commonly called a glitch, develops. A glitch in the tape can weaken any case.

10. All camera movement should be kept to a minimum. Zoom in and out only to follow important movements of the defendant. The clock and calendar should be on camera as much as possible. When a test is being taped in which the defendant is swaying a great deal, the camera should be locked in place on the tripod so that camera movement will not affect the view of the defendant's actions.

11. The closing scene of the taping should be a shot of the defendant standing alongside the clock/calendar. The camera operator should fade out at the end of the taping session. A fade-out is made by slowly turning the camera lens opening back to the c, or closed, position.

Figure 30. Officer is shown adjusting the camera lens prior to videotaping a drunk driver.

110　　　　　　　*Television and Law Enforcement*

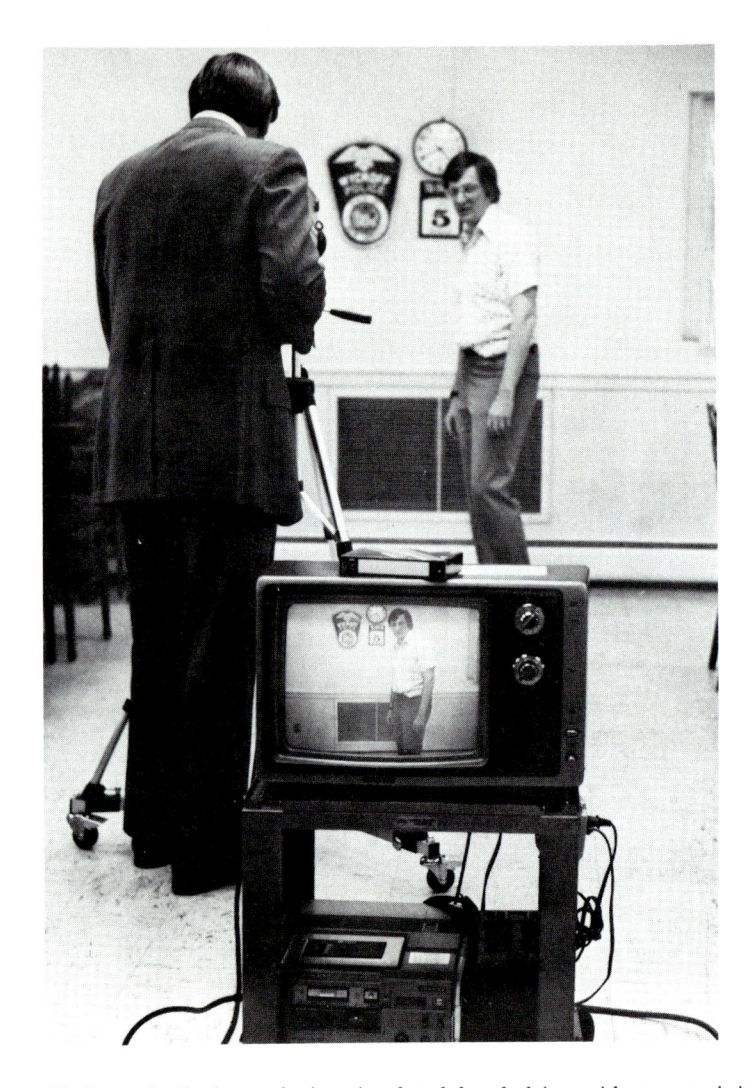

Figure 31. Detective is shown during simulated drunk driver videotape training.

12. The tape should then be stopped, and the ending tape counter numbers noted.
13. When the taping has been completed, the ending numbers should be written on the operator's form along with the total time of taping. The log book must then be completed with all necessary information.

14. The tape recording must then be viewed by the videotape operator so that he can testify that the tape, in fact, represents a true recording of the testing.
15. Only one drunk driver is taped on each tape. This applies even if only ten minutes is used on a two-hour tape. This is important, since questions could arise in court if the tape of one drunk immediately followed that of another. This could put doubt in the mind of the judge, and continuity of evidence could suffer since the tape was used after being logged as evidence. Also, multiple drunks on a tape would prevent erasure if one case was adjudicated before another.
16. The tape is removed from the videorecorder after it has been rewound. Gummed labels should be placed on the tape and the tape sleeve that contain any information required for its identification. This will include the defendant's name, case number, date, and the signature of the videotape operator.
17. The tape will then be placed in a large evidence envelope on which is written the same information as was placed on the tape label. This envelope will then be sealed and placed into an evidence locker. The same rule of the chain of evidence applies to videotape evidence, and it must be adhered to without fail.

Important: Tapes must be stored in a cool, dry location in which there is no strong magnetic field. A strong electromagnetic force can very easily erase all tapes and leave the department in an embarrassing situation.

Normal departmental discovery procedures should be used when showing a tape to a defense attorney or defendant. If possible, tapes should be shown by the officer who operated the videorecorder during the testing procedures. This will easily satisfy the chain of evidence, since he is the only officer who will have opened or sealed the tape.

If it is not possible to have the video operator show the tape, then another certified operator may present the tape for viewing—with certain conditions.

The department should establish before the attorney responds to headquarters to view the tape whether or not he is willing to waive the chain of evidence for that particular tape. If he responds favorably to the request, he will be asked to complete a form that waives the chain of evidence. (A sample of the form is included in Appendix F.)

This form should contain all information such as case number, name of defendant, name of video operator, date of arrest, and officer who is showing the tape. The name and address of the defense attorney and the date of viewing is imperative. The form should have an area in which the attorney will sign that he is waiving the chain of evidence and that the tape was unsealed in his presence. After the tape has been shown, he will be asked to sign to signify that he has viewed the tape and that the tape was resealed in his presence.

This form has virtually eliminated the testimony of the officer who presents the tape for viewing. Most attorneys are willing to waive chain of evidence. If an attorney is not amicable to this waiver, either the operator will have to be called in for overtime if he is working, for example, a midnight shift, or the viewing will have to be scheduled when the officer changes to a shift where viewing will not be a problem.

Remember: It is imperative not to allow an operator other than the one who conducted the taping to show the tape unless a *written* waiver has been obtained.

A procedure must be established for the erasing of the videotapes. Only one officer should be permitted to erase tapes after disposition. This officer will *verify* with the court that the case has been adjudicated. The tape *must* be kept until the time for all appeals has elapsed. Each locality should check with its superior court and prosecutor's office to determine the time allowed for appeal of municipal court decisions. This time is normally at the minimum ten days from the time of conviction. It is recommended that the tapes be kept at least one month so that the time for extraordinary appeals (in which the time for appeal is extended by the court) has elapsed. Once the tape has been erased, the evidence is lost forever.

The tape must be held for any administrative hearing on a

refusal, if required. If a tape is erased prior to these hearings, the department will have to answer to the court why the evidence was destroyed. If the tape is kept for a reasonable time and all efforts are made to keep the tape for the hearings, there should be no problem with the courts. This is why the department must have a stock of videotapes for drunk driving taping. Some tapes may have to be held for over one year until the appeal is scheduled.

The tapes should be erased with a bulk tape eraser. This will prevent wear on the videotape heads if the recorder is used to erase the tapes. The tapes must be *fully* erased prior to their reuse.

Once the tape has been erased, an entry is made in the log book with the erasure information. This includes the signature or initials of the erasing officer along with the date that the tape was erased. The tape can be placed back into service after the erasing is completed.

Videotapes should be taken out of service if there is any problem with the tape cassette or if there is a large amount of dropout on the tape.

It must be stressed to the camera operators that it is their responsibility to prevent damage to the recorder and camera equipment. It is not uncommon to have a belligerent drunk and to have him try to damage the equipment to prevent his being taped. The operator and officer in the taping session should be observant of any problem and take steps to prevent damage.

If a videotape is needed for presentation in court, the videotape operator will have to set up all necessary equipment in the courtroom. The camera is not needed for the playback. The recorder, power supply, and monitor/TV set should be all that is necessary.

The operator will be responsible for the playback of the tape and for returning the equipment to its proper location at the completion of the hearing. A wheeled video cart is handy for bringing the equipment to court and does not necessitate taking apart the equipment, since it can be wheeled to court intact.

One officer should be in charge of equipment maintenance. This includes dusting and cleaning of the camera lens and television screen. The video heads on the recorder must also be periodically cleaned. This should be done by using a nonabrasive head-cleaning cassette (preferably a type such as the Allsop 3®

cassette). The heads should be cleaned in accordance with manufacturer's recommendations, and attempts to clean the heads manually should be avoided. Routine maintenance charts should be developed to enable the officer to establish a maintenance routine.

The equipment should also be serviced by the manufacturer at least every six months. This will include any repairs that are necessary and will keep the recorder belts in shape and the equipment lubricated and serviced.

Departments will find that some defense attorneys request complete copies of their defendant's tapes. If this occurs, the department can copy the tape by using two recorders (see Chapter 9). A fee for this service can be charged, along with the cost of the videotape. If a department has access to only one recorder, the defense attorney can be charged for the cost of renting a second recorder.

Some departments are going one step further in the taping of the drunk driver. They are also conducting the taping on the street. Some departments have actually taped the initial vehicle observation and the resulting roadway testing. These departments have purchased cameras with newvicon tubes and utilize vehicle headlights and spotlights for necessary lighting. Some of the departments then retape the testing at headquarters for a stronger case against the drunk driver.

The departments using on-the-road taping must still follow all standard requirements for taping. Trained operators are still required, and all drunk driving and videotape forms are still required. Even when multiple drunks are arrested, only one drunk suspect can be placed on each tape.

In order to fulfill the requirements of proper audio recording while outdoors, police have used wireless microphones with success. The recorder is powered with a car adaptor or with a battery pack. A monopod (a one-legged tripod that is attached to the bottom of the camera) or a shoulder brace is used to prevent camera movement while taping.

Some departments have purchased or are considering purchasing a van that will roll on any drunk driving arrest and conduct the taping from there. The van is equipped with all of the necessary equipment, and the rear of the van serves as the camera location for stability.

With the constant state of change in the video technology, a highly sensitive camera will soon be developed to tape at night with no auxiliary lighting. The entire camera/recorder will be no larger than the 16 mm cameras of today.

All patrol vehicles may soon be equipped with cameras mounted on the dash to record all traffic violations and stops for evidence in court. New technology has already made available a video camera that contains its own built-in videorecorder. This one-piece unit may find its way into the patrol cars because of its compact size and durability. Only time will tell whether this is to become a reality.

Chapter 14

SURVEILLANCE

Surveillance techniques have changed drastically over the past fifty years due to the many technological advances that have been developed. Before photographic equipment was available, it was often necessary for police departments to use the services of artists to illustrate and record crime scenes. This manner of recording, however, had its limitations. The scene was hand drawn by the artist, and although it portrayed a *representation* of what was present, it was not a true depiction. No matter how proficient an artist was, a drawing could not depict a scene as graphically or as accurately as a photograph.

Traditionally, law enforcement agencies have used still and motion picture photography to record evidence. The introduction of the still camera took the place of the artist and allowed a graphic representation of whatever evidence depiction was needed in court. However, this, too, had its disadvantages. Whenever it was necessary to record the movement of a subject, as is needed for recording the movements of a drunk driver or for recording the traffic movement in a hazardous intersection, the still camera was virtually useless. This problem was solved with the development of the motion picture camera. Many departments were able to purchase 16 mm motion picture cameras for moving photography.

Using the new equipment proved to be troublesome and costly, however. It was learned that an officer who was well versed in the operation of a still camera was not necessarily able to operate a motion picture camera. It was often necessary to give the officer specialized training in the use and operation of the motion picture camera in order for him to be proficient in its use. He had to receive training in the various film types available for use in the camera, exposure computations, camera techniques, and possibly picture development procedures.

Surveillance

The film cameraman was normally limited to a film magazine that contained, at most, 400 feet of film. This would last a maximum of eleven minutes at twenty-four frames per second. The cost of the raw film stock and professional development could well exceed $100.00 for 400 feet.

Since many surveillances take place in low light situations, the officer had a difficult time in computing his exposure. Specialized light meters were necessary in order to read minimum levels of lighting.

The cameraman had no method to determine whether or not the image that he needed was being recorded until the film was developed and viewed, and many departments were unable to develop the motion picture film, since it required specialized equipment, especially if reversal film was being used.

If the film had to be sent out for professional processing, the chain of evidence regarding the film had to be considered. The use of the film was also limited, since it could not be erased and reused.

If the department required color photography, then the cost of the film and its development drastically increased. The development of color film could not normally be accomplished in the department because of the strict development times and temperature controls that have a variance of $\pm 1°F$.

If sound recording on the film was necessary, then the officers had to purchase a film camera that was capable of recording sound on film. A camera of mediocre quality capable of recording sound could cost at least $1,500.00. Magnetically striped film also had to be purchased, which again raised the cost of the filming.

The introduction of videotaping into surveillance documentation has alleviated many of the problems apparent in motion picture photography. It is necessary that the cameraman receive training in the use of the equipment; however, videotape training is not as time consuming as that of training in the use of the motion picture camera.

Depending on the type of videorecorder, the cameraman can have up to eight hours of taping time on one $20.00 videocassette. This recording can also include sound if the proper microphones are used. The sound is automatically synchronized with the visual portion of the recording.

The cameraman is able automatically to see what he is recording in the electronic viewfinder of the camera. If he has a clear image in the finder, this will be recorded on the tape. If his viewfinder is capable of video playback, it provides a means to check his recording for proper stability. It is always wise to run a test tape before recording any situation. This ensures that the recorder is functioning properly.

This test tape has saved many cameramen from embarrassment. It is possible to have all television equipment connected properly and still not record the video or audio signal. A test tape will check the audio– and videorecording to ensure a proper tape. If the audio or video cable is flawed, the test tape will bring the problem to the attention of the video operator and allow him to correct the situation. Many times a faulty cable is to blame, and the solution is to replace the cable with a spare.

Specialized camera tubes are available on the market that will allow taping in low light level situations. The department should *never* use a star light scope on a video camera. The extreme brightness from a scope of this type can burn out small areas of the camera tube or can *completely* burn out the tube. Only the specialized tubes such as the newvicon should be used.

The use of videotape in surveillance has allowed instant playback of the tape upon the camera crew's return to headquarters. There is no lengthy development time, which eliminates another area of cost of a film surveillance. Since most recorders and cameras purchased today are color, the department will have color without the additional expense of using color motion picture film.

Another feature of the videotape that makes financial officers happy is that once the case has been adjudicated, the tape can be erased and reused.

Whenever a surveillance using videotape is to be established, the camera crew must study the area to be taped. The officers must note where the camera is to be placed and check for any lighting that may help or hinder the surveillance. Plans for placement of microphones or transmitters must also be implemented if needed.

It is good to remember that if the department has access to body transmitters, the receiving unit can be plugged directly into the microphone input of the videorecorder. This will allow audio signals to be transmitted directly to the recorder. This is very useful in recording a drug buy in which an undercover officer is wired.

The most important question that must be answered on this study must be what type of lens to use for the situation. Most surveillances will be taped a distance from the subject; thus, a telephoto lens of some type must be utilized. As discussed in previous chapters, a telephoto lens for a video camera is normally any lens above 12.5 mm.

It is suggested that the department purchase a camera with a C-mount fitting, since this is the standard fitting that has been used for years on 16 mm film cameras. Many lenses in various focal lengths have been manufactured for the film cameras, and these can be used on the video cameras. The wide assortment available offers many price differences; however, the more expensive lenses normally offer better resolution and definition.

An invaluable piece of equipment for any surveillance team is an adaptor that enables a 35 mm still camera lens to be used on a video camera. If your department uses a Minolta® camera, an adaptor can be purchased that converts the Minolta fitting to a C-mount fitting. This adaptor can normally be purchased for under $60.00 and can be found in any well-equipped camera shop. This adaptor has another feature. If one were to place a 50 mm lens on the video camera by using this adaptor, the lens would, in effect, become a 100 mm lens on the video camera. The adaptor will double the focal length of any lens normally used on a 35 mm format camera. The lens is placed on the adaptor and is then fitted to the video camera. If one were to use a 75 mm to 150 mm zoom telephoto lens for the Minolta, it becomes a 150 mm to 300 mm lens on the video camera.

Another very handy gadget for use with the C-mount adaptor is a $2\times$ or $3\times$ tele-extender that is made for the 35 mm camera. A tele-extender either doubles ($2\times$) or triples ($3\times$) the focal length of a lens. If the tele-extender is used between the 35 mm lens and the C-mount adaptor, the lens is transformed into a powerful telephoto.

Using the example of the 75 mm to 150 mm lens combined with

the tele-extender and the C-mount adaptor, the lens becomes a 300 mm to 600 mm lens with the 2× tele-extender. With the 3× tele-extender it becomes a 450 mm to 900 mm lens.

The only drawback to the use of these adaptors is that the light-gathering capability of the lens is decreased. In low light situations this may not be desirable. In this case, a normal C-mount lens can be used to gather as much light as possible.

The adaptor can be used with any video camera that has a manual or auto-iris lens. The only difference is that the cameraman will have to adjust the light level by using the manual f-stops on an auto-iris lens rather than having it adjusted automatically by the auto-iris.

Whenever a lens above a 200 mm focal length is placed on the camera, a tripod must be used. Camera movements are extremely magnified when a long lens is used. A slight jarring of the camera can completely remove the surveillance subject from the viewfinder. It is virtually impossible to hold the camera steady with a long lens without using a tripod.

Once all of the equipment has been selected and the camera placed into position, the task of waiting begins. It is wise to keep spare batteries for the recorder handy that will last the entire time of the surveillance. Many batteries will last approximately ninety minutes with the camera and recorder in operation. A team on an eight-hour surveillance should have at least nine batteries on the scene. The job is made much easier if the location of the camera setup is equipped with electricity.

If a surveillance is being made from an automobile, a power adaptor that is plugged into the cigarette lighter of the car is available, which will power the recorder and camera from the battery of the car. Manufacturers recommend that the car engine be running when this is in use; however, it can be used for a short time with the engine off, and the results will be satisfactory.

The taping officers must be sure to take all of the necessary connecting cables that will be needed for the recorder, camera, and any audiorecording equipment. If even one wire is forgotten, it can put a complete halt to the taping.

The camera should always be left in the on position. This will eliminate any warm-up time that may be required if the camera is needed immediately. The recorder can be kept off, since it can be immediately started if needed for taping. It is *imperative* that the officer make sure that he triggers the switch on the camera that will start the tape moving. Many a surveillance tape has been missed because the trigger was never depressed and the tape never started. A visual inspection of the recorder should be quickly made to be sure that the tape has started rolling and is properly working. This will save the embarrassment of a "Dear Chief" letter explaining why nothing was taped. Since many departments require still photographs of a surveillance, this can be accomplished by using only the video camera and recorder.

After a surveillance is over, it may be necessary to produce still photographs from the videotaped surveillance. These may be required for suspect identification or for passing out at roll call. It is a simple procedure to photograph an image from a television screen from a videotape. The only equipment needed is a still camera with a shutter speed of 1/8 to 1/15 of a second and a sturdy tripod.

Since the videotape is shown at a speed of thirty frames per second, a photograph from the screen must be taken at a shutter speed of 1/8 or 1/30 of a second, which will help to eliminate the black scanning lines that may block out portions of the photograph. A camera with a leaf shutter should be used. The photographer should take at least five shots of the scene that he requires at different exposures to ensure that the scanning lines will be eliminated.

The procedure for photographing from screen is as follows:

1. The camera operator should place the television set in a darkened room and play back the videotape. He should *not* use a flash or auxiliary lighting. The picture contrast should be adjusted for a medium to soft picture.
2. The operator should position the camera in front of the television screen and focus on the screen as sharply as possible. It is a good idea to use a tripod.
3. The operator should adjust the camera f-stop to coincide with the shutter speed that will produce the correct exposure.
4. If necessary, one can photograph a portion of the screen. For

example, a photograph can be taken of the subject standing outside of a building and the camera can be moved so that only the subject appears in the photograph. It must be pointed out that picture clarity will decrease when photographs are taken from sections of the television screen.

Once the still photograph is taken, enlargements can be made and distributed.

It is important to remember that there is a place in surveillance for still photography. Videotaping should normally be used when *motion* recording of a subject is needed. For example, the following instances would be clearer using videotape: (1) taping an undercover officer making a drug buy from a suspect and (2) taping an actual commission of a crime or taping civil disturbances in which the participants will have to be identified and prosecuted for their actions.

The camera operator can use his ingenuity in taping various situations. Depending on local laws and procedures, it is possible to borrow various cameraman garments from local television studios. Most individuals will not question a person operating a video camera who is garbed in the clothing of a television studio. The studio should be made aware of the purpose that the borrowed clothing will be used for, and it must be used for that purpose alone. This will ensure future cooperation with the studio.

It is also helpful to use a nondescript van that is fitted with one-way mirrors. This allows freedom of movement for the camera personnel, and their activities will not be noticed. It is very important to have the vehicle properly heated and air-conditioned both for the comfort of the crew and the well-being of the videotape. A temperature of approximately 70°F is suggested to prolong the life of the videotape.

A department should try not to use a video surveillance when a photographic surveillance will suffice. Many times a department will use equipment that is not really justified for a specific purpose. If stills will do the job, then still pictures should be used. Equipment can wear out with overuse and should only be used when the situation warrants it.

Chapter 15

DEPARTMENTAL TRAINING

Departmental training with the use of films or slides is limited due to a number of factors. Many departments are unable to allocate the monies necessary to purchase police training films, which normally cost about $400.00 and up. Even when the films have been purchased, many times they are not in line with various state laws or show procedures that conflict with those of the department. Such films also become outdated rapidly. It is very difficult to show a film with 1950 automobiles and procedures and have it taken seriously by the audience.

Slide presentations have also suffered from the same drawbacks, since the audiovisual aids have been produced to sell to departments across the country and may contain policies that do not apply to a particular department. They also become outdated quickly, since scenery and vehicle styles frequently change.

Inasmuch as filmmakers are unable to satisfy everyone because of the diversity of laws and procedures, some of the larger police departments have attempted to produce their own training films or tapes. Most of their work has been in the production of roll call training tapes. These were short (maximum of ten minutes) films or tapes that were normally shown to the audience during roll calls. They covered various areas of concern, such as handcuffing techniques, searching techniques, care of the service revolver, and other subjects that are only limited by the imagination of the producer.

One positive feature of using roll call training tapes is that the student is able to review the material on the tape at his leisure even after the initial presentation. This enables him to brush up on material in which he may require additional study time.

Until recently, the cost of producing this type of training aid was exorbitant and normally out of the range of the smaller department. The development of easy-to-use equipment and the tremendous price reductions have allowed departments to enter the field of production. Video equipment has enabled many small departments to prepare their own departmental training tapes. The extreme ease with which the production can be accomplished has brought forth training tapes that are relevant to particular departmental needs. Not only will a departmentally produced training tape be relevant, it will also give the student a point of reference, since it will be taped in the area of his jurisdiction and will give him more empathy with the production.

A department with a single camera/recorder will be able to produce tapes that will be semiprofessional by shooting the tape in sequence. Normally, the professional filmmaker shoots the entire film out of sequence. He will, for example, shoot all outdoor location shots at one time, even though he may be only shooting the beginning and end of the film. He will then edit the film in the proper sequence once the filming has been completed.

When shooting a production completely in sequence (also called editing in camera), the producer/director *must* develop a script that will spell out the entire production. It will give instructions to the cameraman and actors and will present all necessary shooting information. It is normally divided into a section on one side of the page for *video* and one side of the page for *audio*. This will enable the production crew to know which areas of the taping require audio or voice-overs and which sections require a music score. Scripting is necessary whether one camera/recorder is used or ten cameras/recorders are used.

If a department is fortunate enough to own a two camera/recorder system, then the shooting may be done out of sequence and later electronically edited. The ultimate production system would be composed of two color cameras, two video recorders, and an electronic editing system. This setup would produce the most professional results without glitches or editing flaws.

Some steps necessary for a worthwhile production follow:

1. *Developing the subject to be presented.* It is imperative that the subject be fully researched before a script is written. Textbooks on the subject, along with departmental procedures, must be examined. Personnel in the department with expertise in the subject area

should also be consulted for ideas to be presented. The most important aspect of the production is that the material presented be correct. Improper or incorrect material will completely negate the positive aspects of the videotape training.

2. *Selecting the material and scripting.* Once the material for presentation has been researched, the next step is to write the script. As mentioned previously, the script should contain instruction to the crew and actors. Ad-libbing by the actors should be kept to a minimum so that the material is correct in its presentation. The script should be written with the audience in mind. If the tape is to be presented to raw recruits, then the material and manner of presentation should be geared to their level of competence.

Locations selected for shooting should be cleared for taping by the producer prior to the arrival of the crew. This may necessitate the producer's obtaining permission from the owner of the property, securing the necessary insurance, and possibly obtaining shooting permits. If a street location is to be closed to the public, the producer may have to obtain permission from the governing body of the town and county.

Any props that will be needed should be obtained to ensure that they will be ready when needed.

Makeup requirements or special effects (such as blank ammunition or stage blood) should be arranged prior to taping. It is important to remember that actors may need makeup for regular shooting. Even if a male actor is well shaven, the camera may make his face look as if he has not shaved. Simple use of pancake makeup (available in most drugstores) will eliminate any facial shadow when properly applied.

3. *Selecting actors.* After the script has been finished, the selection of the actors will then take place. Most actors can be found within the confines of the police department, since many aspects of law enforcement require that the officer be an actor of sorts.

It is important that the actor(s) be convincing in their roles, since many productions have been hampered by actors who tend to overplay the role. When this occurs, the training tape can become a comedy instead of a learning experience. The producer should have the actors read for the part to ascertain whether or not they will be appropriate. Friendship should have no place in the selection of actors—only their ability should be a part in their selection.

The actors should be given their scripts far enough in advance of production so that they will be able to memorize their parts. Several dress rehearsals should be held so that any problems can be ironed out before taping.

4. *Setting up production.* Once the scripting has been finished and the actors have been selected, along with the taping locations, the production can be started. The producer/director should select and gather all equipment necessary for the shooting. He must be sure that all equipment is in proper working order and that all necessary auxiliary equipment is present.

Transportation for equipment and crew should be arranged. Weather conditions can destroy an outdoor sequence, so alternate shooting sequences should be provided for in the case of inclement weather.

5. *Taping the production.* If titles are to be utilized, a very simple device can be made to simulate a television crawl effectively. This device will allow letters to roll up the television screen as is done on professional television productions. The letters cannot be superimposed, however, without special effects equipment. (See Chapter 6 for detailed instructions on making a crawl and Chapter 10 for alternative methods used for Lettering.)

Once the crawl device has been manufactured, the cameraman merely shoots the copy with a close-up lens, and the crawl will fill the screen.

The crawl also has another use if a department is fortunate enough to own two recorders. If a production calls for an on-camera announcer, the crawl can be used as a teleprompter. A teleprompter is used on commercial networks so that the announcer will not have to memorize his script. The teleprompter is a device that allows the lines for the announcer to be placed in front of the camera and rolled at whatever rate the speaker requires.

This can be duplicated in a departmental production by typing the announcer's lines on the roll of paper for the crawl device. The copy is then rolled for the person who will serve as the announcer. The announcer will read at his own pace, and as he is reading his lines, the crawl will be videotaped. Once the crawl has been taped, the announcer can read the lines from a television set that is placed directly below the camera that tapes the announcer. The announcer will appear on camera to be reciting his lines from memory. He will, in fact, be reading his lines from the teleprompter that does not appear on camera.

Once the initial titles have been finished, the production will move to the location shooting. The tape should be reviewed after each take to ensure that the taping is satisfactory. A log should be kept to show which scenes have been shot and what their durations are. This will help the production stay on schedule.

One thing that is *imperative* in any production is proper reinforcement of correct actions. Many times a training tape will show the incorrect, as well as the correct, actions to take in a given situation. When this type of training is presented, it is important to remember that the correct way must be shown last. The correct way will then, it is hoped, stay in the student's mind, since it will be the last thing that he sees on the screen.

6. *Supplementing commercial training films.* Many departments have utilized a shoot/don't shoot training film. One particularly good film is available from Motorola. It is possible for departments to supplement this training film with a videotape of their own for training purposes. A department can videotape several vignettes in their own jurisdiction. Locations such as banks, stores, or residential dwellings can be used to develop a shoot/don't shoot tape for their officers.

Most videorecorders have a still or pause control that will stop the videotape when depressed. This control can be used as the trigger of a gun for training purposes. The officer can view the tape in the presence of the instructor. If and when he feels that it is necessary to fire his weapon, he can depress the still/pause button on the recorder. He will in theory have fired his weapon. The instructor can then discuss his actions, and evaluation can be made of the student.

Once again, the training tape will be only as limited as the imagination of the producer/director. The subject matter is almost unlimited. If enough thought and effort go into the production, it can be a project from which everyone will benefit.

Chapter 16

TRAFFIC

Videorecording can be a useful and efficient tool in the area of traffic enforcement, surveys, and planning. Much of the work of the traffic officer is comprised of examining traffic locations for enforcement purposes or for evaluation of existing traffic regulations for change. He must select locations for radar enforcement and other necessary traffic details.

When a group of residents complain that the timing of a traffic signal is causing a backup of traffic, the traffic officer must examine the intersection and evaluate the complaint. Many times, he will have to submit his recommendations to a higher authority for action. If the traffic officer were to videotape the intersection during the times of examination, he would have a visual presentation to confirm or to deny the request for change. It would also give him a visual representation that can be examined at leisure by his superiors.

Videotape recordings can also be used to sell the town or state on needed changes or improvements in the traffic officer's jurisdiction. He can put together a tape of trouble spots that will enhance his presentation. Close-ups of engineering faults can be shot along with vehicles experiencing trouble at a specific location. The traffic officer has the option of mounting the camera in the patrol vehicle with a tripod or hand holding his camera.

Traffic counts can be accomplished by using videotape without the continued presence of an officer. A recorder can be set up at the required location either in a vehicle or a home near the location. The tape can be started with the camera focused on the traffic count location. The recorder can be left on, and the officer can leave the location. Depending on the length of the tape and the type of equipment used, the officer will only have to return to change tapes or to retrieve his equipment. Once the tape has been made, he can return to headquarters, and by using the forward search (if present on the department's recorder), he will be able to count his vehicles in record time.

Traffic flow studies can also be taped, which will have bearing on the future traffic requirements of the community.

Many times traffic officers will have to comment on site plans for the planning board of their locality. A videotaped survey of the location can help them to make their determination of traffic problems and will be useful in a presentation to the planning board.

It is possible to have a mount installed on the dashboard of the traffic unit, which enables the camera to be in use when the traffic car is in motion. This can then be used prior to and during a traffic stop. The tape showing the violation can then be shown to the defendant and possibly can be used in court. Each jurisdiction must check local and state judicial decisions for using this type of tape in the courtroom, since no federal case law has been decided on this subject.

If the traffic officer is called to a serious motor vehicle accident, he can videotape the scene and the approaches of the accident vehicle. This can be used to supplement still photographs of the scene. If color tape is used, the tape should not show scenes that may be considered shocking to the jurors. If a quantity of blood or gore is present and a color camera is being used, the color can be turned off on the monitor when played back. The same standards for jury presentation should be applicable for videotaped evidence at the accident scene.

As with still photography, taping should take place from all points of view. The tape is not made just to show damage but to show viewpoints of drivers, passengers, and witnesses. The camera should be positioned at the level of view of each party. For example, the camera operator should measure the distance from the ground to the driver's window of each vehicle and position his camera at the correct level of view. If the driver of vehicle number one is 5 feet from ground level, then the camera operator should position his tripod at this height and move his camera accordingly.

Viewpoint taping should be conducted for *each* person involved in the accident or for witnesses. Many times a witness will claim to have seen the entire event. When the perspective of the viewer is checked, it can be determined whether it was physically possible for the witness to have seen what has been claimed.

Many patrol officers will photograph only damage on the accident vehicles. This may assist the traffic investigator in reconstructing the accident; however, it is *not* the only photograph or tape to be recorded. It is important that the camera operator be fully trained in the field of traffic accident investigation so that he will be aware of what is to be recorded.

It is as important, if not more so, to prevent accidents as well as to determine their causes. The traffic officer can also use the videotape in his traffic safety program. Tapes of bicycle safety, pedestrian safety, and so forth can be used during his lectures or used for cable television.

Many jurisdictions, including New Jersey, have been faced with the recent enactment of laws that allow mopeds to be operated on the roadway. It has been the experience in New Jersey that the public is not informed concerning the new laws that have been enacted. This lack of knowledge has led to many individuals' operating the moped illegally. Videotaped educational programs on this subject can help to educate the public and to keep them informed on any changes in the law. Informational videotapes of this kind may be used in any area of the motor vehicle code in which major changes have developed. This subject will be discussed more fully in Chapter 20, "Public Relations."

It must be stressed that the traffic officer can utilize the videorecorder in many other ways, such as training his officers to use radar. The training procedure with videotape should be developed with the consultation of the department training officer and video producer.

The traffic officer can also videotape his men while on traffic control duty and then critique the officers' directing techniques at a later time. This will enable officers on traffic duty to see their own performance while on post.

With the constant changes in the duties of traffic officers, they must strive for professionalism. One method of establishing this professionalism is to keep up to date with technological changes. Using videotape is but one area of modernization of the traffic bureau.

Chapter 17

TAPING OF MAJOR CRIME SCENES

Whenever a crime of major significance occurs in a locality, the police department will normally photograph the crime scene with a still camera. If the situation warrants it, the department may use color film to record the evidence.

With the advent of the portable color video equipment, some departments have begun to videotape major crime scenes, in addition to photographing them. The videotaping can serve the investigating officer in ways that still photography is limited. Videotaping allows the officer a virtually unlimited field of movement that allows him to follow the crime scene from the beginning to the end.

If there is a supervising investigative agency such as the prosecutor's office or district attorney, the department should obtain permission to tape the crime scene. Once the preliminary investigation is complete and the initial facts are known, the investigating officer may then videotape the scene.

It is suggested that the officer videotape the perimeter of the scene before entering the crime scene area. This will enable him to view the tape for any information that could have been missed on the preliminary investigation. This may require additional lighting. Many police departments will find the local fire department of immense help in lighting crime scene areas. Emergency fire trucks usually contain floodlights, which can be brought to the scene to provide the light necessary for clear videotapes.

While taping, the officer should narrate the scene using the built-in camera microphone. His observations will therefore be synchronized with the scene recorded. This will eliminate the need for copious notes while recording. The taping officer should give his name, rank, case number, date, and location at the start of the videotape.

After the perimeter taping is complete, the officer should then enter the scene *in the manner that the perpetrator gained entry.* This is not to say that if the perpetrator entered a home by breaking a pane of glass in the door the officer should break another pane. He should enter by the same point of entry and attempt to follow the actions of the perpetrator.

The cameraman should take close-up shots of any important evidence and its relation to other evidence in the room. In the situation of a homicide, positions of the bodies should be taped along with any evidence in their surrounding areas. An officer who is taping a homicide will not have to worry about the color taping being prejudicial to the jury. Even though the taping is in color, the officer can make the playback in black and white simply by turning off the color controls on the playback television set.

After the actual crime scene rooms have been taped, the officer should also tape the rooms that have not been disturbed. This will preserve the entire scene in the house for future study and is particularly helpful if additional investigation proves that the undisturbed rooms may have some evidentiary value.

Since most videotapes will last a minimum of two hours (depending on the equipment and tape used), the officer should have enough tape to cover most situations. The cost of the videotape is normally less than that of photographing the entire scene.

The same rules of evidence that apply to videotaping a crime scene are applicable to photographing the scene. The videotape, along with the photographs, can help piece together what transpired during the crime. The officer can use the tape in court on a large screen television set for the jury rather than pass photographs to the jurors.

It should be remembered that photographs can be taken from the television screen for additional courtroom presentation. (See Chapter 14 for details on photographing a television picture.) Videotaped witness statements can be used to supplement the case further. These statements can be taken directly at the scene and will help prevent the witness's memory loss while being transported to headquarters for a statement.

It is important to remember that videotaping the scene is *in addition to* still photography. It is a supplementary tool and should not replace present means of recording evidence. As of this writing, the United States Supreme Court has not decided on videotape admissibility for crime scenes. At this time, admissibility varies from state to state and federal district to federal district. Until the Supreme Court rules, police should exercise common sense in using the equipment and develop procedures that will not allow the tape to be declared inadmissible. As long as officers are aware of the rights of the accused and make every effort to use videotape within the rules of evidence as they now exist, it should be difficult to have a tape suppressed in a hearing.

Videotape will always be an *auxiliary* tool for law enforcement. It can never replace the investigator or his standard tools of investigation, such as common sense, witness interviews, fingerprint examination, leg work, and other scientific means of investigation. No machine will *ever* replace the properly trained investigator.

Chapter 18

TAPING OF CONFESSIONS

It has been common practice for police officers to use some means of recording confessions of persons suspected of crimes. Recording has been in the form of handwritten statements, typed confessions, audiorecordings of confessions, and, recently, videotaped confessions.

A videotaped confession is a very credible means to show that a confession was made voluntarily and freely. The judge and jury are able to view the defendant while he presents his confession and are able to observe his demeanor and condition at the time the recording was made.

Certain guidelines should be followed when videotaping a confession. In all cases where a confession is to be taped, permission should be obtained from the prosecutor's office or the district attorney's office.

1. The videotaped confession should only be used in cases of major importance. Guidelines for the taping should be developed by each department and placed in the procedure book of the taping department. A polygraph examination is not used for every case a department has, nor should a confession be taped for every case.

2. An appropriate room should be selected for taping. No interruptions can be allowed once the taping begins. The room should contain, at the minimum, a chair for the defendant and a table for him to sit behind. If an officer is to be present in the room in addition to the cameraman, he should also be on camera. The room must contain an accurate clock, which is positioned so that it is on camera at all times during the confession. A calendar indicating the correct day should also be near the clock. A good location to position these items is on the wall behind the suspect so that both he and the clock/calendar are on camera at all times.

An auxiliary microphone should be used to provide a clear and concise recording and to eliminate any unnecessary noises. The lighting in the room should be sufficient to obtain a good picture, and auxiliary lighting should be positioned to provide necessary illumination.

Once the taping has started, the tape must not be stopped for any reason other than equipment breakdown. Even this stoppage will have to be explained in court.

3. The taping can be done in many ways. Initial questioning of the suspect should not be taped. The only thing that should be taped is the actual statement or confession of the suspect. The suspect should be sworn in on camera, and the normal questions about name, address, and the like should be asked. The suspect *may* again be read his rights on camera and asked whether the confession is free and voluntary with no promises or guarantees made to him. Of course, this will be at least the second time that the suspect has been read his rights. The suspect can either read his handwritten or typed statement/confession into the camera or the questioning officer can read him questions on camera. It should be kept in mind that this is *not* the fact-finding questioning, since the questioning officer will have elicited a confession before this taping takes place. The taped confession is an additional piece of evidence for the prosecution and *will never* take the place of a typed or handwritten confession. Many times, a stenographer will already have transcribed the suspect's confession, and he can read the transcription on camera, providing that it was properly obtained and transcribed.

Some agencies have not taped their major confessions, saying that this hampers the confession of a suspect. They say that many times the suspect will write a statement but be unwilling to do so on camera. They also feel that taping the confession gives the defense attorney another area to attack.

If a suspect refuses to give a statement on camera but will do so on audiorecordings, the department should by all means take the statement on audio. If the interrogator still wishes to tape the suspect after his refusal to appear on camera, he can tape the suspect on the refusal, and it will show the demeanor of the suspect in court.

If a confession is properly obtained, the taping process should not be the subject of an attack by a defense attorney. This is only a *supplement* to the handwritten, typed, or transcribed confession and does not take its place. Since the use of videotape in this area of law enforcement is rather new, the court decisions on its use will have to be carefully examined in order to determine its true effectiveness. Until that time, if it is used properly and correctly, its use should not be ignored.

Chapter 19

CLOSED-CIRCUIT TELEVISION

Many police agencies have begun to utilize closed-circuit television (CCTV) for departmental security or for monitoring high crime areas. This equipment is, in effect, a small scale television station.

Closed-circuit cameras are set up to send a video signal to a television set at a monitoring station. The cameras are normally black and white and are powered by a 9-volt power supply that runs off AC house current. The cameras are lightweight and can be purchased with many features, depending on their intended uses.

Cameras can be purchased with either a vidicon or newvicon tube. The vidicon tube does not provide a sharp image at night or when the area is not well lit, and the tube tends to burn in when a constant light source strikes it. A newvicon tube, coupled with an auto-iris lens is much more sensitive to night light and is not as sensitive to burn-in or lag. Neither tube will function in total darkness, and an auxiliary light source is needed to illuminate the area of concern.

When the camera is positioned outdoors, a camera housing is needed to protect the camera. The housing is shatterproof and is weather resistant. It can be purchased with a cooling fan or a heating element for locations where temperature extremes are prevalent.

The housing can be mounted on remote-controlled brackets that can be moved vertically or horizontally so that the monitoring station can vary the camera angle. A remote controlled lens that will enable the monitoring station to zoom in and out can also be purchased. This will give the camera operator almost unlimited movement and view of the monitored area. If a camera is used to monitor hallways in the police station, the camera housing can be eliminated, and the camera mounted on a bracket.

The television monitor is usually a special black and white monitor that allows direct cable connection to the video camera. The direct feed will provide an exceptionally sharp picture on the screen. The monitor is usually no more that 12 inches, and cases are available that allow monitors to be mounted next to each other.

It is possible to have multiple cameras hooked up to one or more television sets at the monitoring station. If multiple cameras are hooked up to one set, it can be set up so that the officer manning the station can select which camera signal will appear on the monitor. It is also possible to have a scan set up, which will show views from each camera in sequence on the screen for a selected period of time. The image from camera 1 will be on the screen first for ten seconds, then the image from camera 2 for ten seconds, and so on. This timing sequence can be varied from shorter to longer times depending on the needs of the agency. If the officer spots trouble during the scan, he can punch up that camera for a constant video image.

If a recorded image is desired, a videorecorder can be hooked up that will begin recording the video image when the recorder is started. The video cameras can also be hooked up to a distribution console that will enable each camera to feed into its own monitor. This is more expensive than the single monitor but allows constant views of each scene from each camera.

Many banking establishments have begun to use videotape recording in the place of their film recorders. Multiple cameras are set up and are fed into one or more monitors. The cameras are scanned at a constant rate, and the images are fed to the monitors. A time-lapse videorecorder is hooked up to one monitor, and constant recordings at several frames per second are made. In the event that a holdup takes place and the alarm is sounded, the recorder begins taping at normal speed to record the scene.

CCTV has been used in police agencies to monitor the exterior of the police station, the cell areas, and hallways and doorways leading to the police area. Since there is normally only one officer in headquarters in many smaller departments, the video camera gives him security at headquarters, since he can view the outside of the building for problems and can check individuals who are entering headquarters. Many times the only person in headquarters is a dispatcher, and video cameras can allow him time to call an officer into headquarters if he observes a problem arising.

The CCTV in the cell area of headquarters will allow the desk officer to monitor the actions of the prisoner constantly. If the desk officer/dispatcher is alone in headquarters, it is sometimes difficult for him to leave his duty station to check on prisoners. The CCTV will allow him to be alert for suicide attempts or illness of prisoners. This simple viewing setup can help to eliminate a lawsuit if a prisoner commits suicide in the cell, since his actions are under constant monitoring.

Video cameras have also been used by some departments to monitor coastal shore areas. CCTV has been set up at locations on boardwalks in high crime areas. The cameras are mounted on poles at distances along the boardwalk, and an officer at headquarters monitors the signals to determine whether police actions are warranted.

The CCTV has also been used to monitor the interiors of the tunnels that lead from New Jersey to New York, which are owned by the Port Authority of New York and New Jersey. The cameras are set at fixed locations throughout the tunnels to monitor traffic flow or problems. This prevents individuals from having to patrol the interior of the tunnels on foot and has decreased manpower needs for patrolling.

Store security has been using CCTV for many years, and the results have been very satisfactory. It allows limited security personnel to monitor the store from a central location.

The newly erected casinos in New Jersey have designed a complex CCTV system within the casinos. Cameras are located in the ceilings of the casinos and permit a view of gambling tables. This is to help deter customer cheating and to monitor licensed employees. The cameras are located in decorative one-way glass domes above the table locations, and the cameras are invisible to individuals who are not familiar with the setup.

CCTV is extremely useful in monitoring locations where it is difficult to station an officer or watchman. It gives the officer another set of eyes to ensure that if a problem develops, he will be aware of its existence.

Chapter 20

PUBLIC RELATIONS

The police administrator of today has become more cognizant of the need for a well-developed public relations program. With the disappearance of the foot patrolman, the public has had very limited contact with the police. People normally only see police when the need arises for service. Many times citizens meet officers at traumatic times in their lives, and this may be the only face-to-face contact that will take place in their lifetimes. The officer in the patrol car may be highly visible; however, the personalized contact with the public is missing.

To help rectify this situation, many departments have started complex public relations programs. These programs have been comprised of school lectures, lectures to civic groups, fingerprinting of school children to aid in their identification in the event that they are missing, crime prevention programs, traffic safety programs, and even citizen crime watch programs. These programs place the police officer in the forefront of these community groups. He is no longer an unknown man in blue but a man with a name. The overwhelming success of the programs has forced the police administrator to look for ways to keep the officer before the public as much as is possible without stripping his essential patrol force.

One manner of making the officers more visible has been through the use of videotaped programming. There are two main methods used in departmentally produced programming—videotape libraries maintained by the law enforcement agency for use by the public and broadcasts of videotapes through local cable channels.

Most school systems and many civic groups have access to videotape recorders or players. This means that a videotape can be used to supplement an officer's presentation, or it can be used in the officer's absence.

The police department can have a library of videotapes on a

variety of subjects that will be of interest to various viewers. The tapes should be produced with the audience in mind. For example, tapes should be produced based on the age group and concerns of the specific audience. If a tape is to be made on crime prevention for grades 1 through 5, the subject matter and its presentation will be drastically different than for a tape for the Rotary Club of a township. The tape cannot be used to replace the personal contact of the officer; however, it can be used before his scheduled lecture date so that the audience can then prepare questions on the subject matter that was presented.

Another method of presentation is through the cable system of a locality. Over the past five years, cable television has made drastic inroads into the broadcasting market. Many localities have contracted with or are in the process of contracting with cable companies for their programming.

The majority of companies have channels for the use of governmental agencies. These channels are for the use of the towns that are being served by the cable company. The only expense to the town is for a demodulator, which normally costs in the area of $2,000.00. This is a one-time expense and enables the town to broadcast on its local access channel. This enables a variety of programming to originate from the governing body or its various agencies. Many towns will broadcast the town meetings over the cable system along with tapes produced by the police department.

The police department is virtually unlimited in the programming it can produce. The subject matter can range from tapes on bicycle safety to tapes on purchasing a lock for home security. The public has been very receptive to this type of programming, since many residents are unable to attend lectures by the police department.

Not only will these presentations enhance the public relations image of the department, but they will also assist the department in having their officers made known to the public. Many departments are faced with a situation in which officers are totally unknown to the general public. Presentations will help to eliminate the public's feeling that police officers are only a blue blur in a police car.

It must be remembered that each program must be fully scripted so that the proper information is presented. A great deal of thought should go into the presentations so that a truly professional image is presented to the public. It is a good idea to begin all shows in the same manner. A close-up of the departmental patch or car emblem along with the department's telephone number is a suggestion for opening every show.

A music score over the tape makes the show more professional. Whenever a musical score is used that is not original, permission *must* be received from the copyright owner. This will prevent any lawsuits that can result from using copyrighted material without permission. Many owners will give permission without charge if the piece will be used in an educational presentation.

It is also wise to obtain model releases from all actors in the show, even departmental personnel. Again, this can prevent legal ramifications in the event that an officer leaves the department and does not want his material in the tape presented. (A sample release is shown in Appendix B.)

Many departments have used actors from their locality. This will give the public a feeling that they are a part of the law enforcement effort, and they will tend to advertise the tape to their friends and neighbors.

Public relations is one of the most important aspects of the police role. Without the support of the public, the police department loses most of its eyes and ears. With manpower shortages coupled with budgetary limitations, police need all of the help possible to complete their difficult tasks.

Chapter 21

OTHER USES OF VIDEOTAPE

Videotape recordings can be used in various areas of criminal justice. These will be mentioned briefly in order to present other methods of usage that may have been considered specialized.

Videotape can be used within the court system in different ways. The first and most widely developed use of videotape is for the recording of depositions. A deposition is a sworn statement containing the testimony of a witness that is to be used at a trial. Normally a deposition is recorded by a stenographer, and the statement is used in court in various ways.

A deposition may be used by either side of the judicial system to impugn the testimony of a witness. For example, if a witness makes a statement during his deposition that he was home on a certain night and during his courtroom testimony he claims that he was at a friend's house on the night in question, the deposition can be used to contradict his testimony.

The court may also order that a deposition be taken from an individual who is physically incapable of attending the trial and whose testimony is crucial. The videotaped deposition can be used in lieu of or in addition to any written or transcribed statement from that witness. In the event that an individual is near death, the court can also order his or her deposition to be taken for use in court.

The videotape can also be used while taking standard depositions prior to trial. Since attorneys representing both sides are normally present during the taking of a deposition, there is no problem in recording the statement by videotape.

Attorneys have also been using videotape for the recording of wills and other legal documents. It is very difficult for an individual to contest a videotaped will, since the mental and physical status of the writer is present for all to see.

Some judicial systems have also recorded the complete jury trial for showing to a jury at a later date or to supplement stenographic recording. The courts are also in the process of using the videotape recordings for training purposes for new prosecutors and defense attorneys.

The use of television for courtroom security cannot be overlooked, since it can furnish court officers with additional views of the courtroom and its entrances and exits.

Law enforcement officers can also use the videotape recorder for recording public demonstrations or riots. The recordings can be made for both evidentiary and training purposes. During the actual occurrence, the tape can be used for recording unlawful acts that are committed by individuals who are participants in the demonstration or riot. It is very useful to record the actual offenses such as theft, malicious mischief, and arson. The tape can also be used to identify unknown participants.

It is very important that the camera be protected from violence during civil disturbances. Many departments have purchased special vans for this use. These vehicles are usually heavily armored and protected and are excellent for the placement of the video equipment. The unit can be positioned behind one-way bulletproof glass. This will afford both protection and secrecy for the recordings.

The recordings will also be useful for the police administrator to ensure that the proper police actions were taken. It will enable him to determine whether the response was correct and whether the plan of action was correct. Examination will show whether there were tactical errors that delayed control of the situation and will enable him to correct the deficiencies. It will also assist him in locating the strong points of the response and allow him to strengthen any weak points. Departmental training officers can then utilize the recordings for both recruit and in-service training classes.

Another area in which law enforcement can use videotape is in the execution of a search warrant. Strict guidelines for the execution of a warrant have been set by the courts, and videotape can prove that all guidelines have been followed.

The search warrant will specify the areas that can be searched by the officers. The taping officer can follow the participants of the search and record their actions. Normally, one officer serves as the recording officer, whose function is to document where and by whom the evidence was found. The videotape officer can record the entire search of the scene, and this can be used to transcribe the search to paper. The tape will supplement any written reports of the officers.

Videotape can also be used for lineups. The tape can be used as a substitute for an actual lineup or to ensure compliance with the *Wade* decision and other landmark cases involving lineups. Decisions on lineups, such as *United States v. Wade*,[1] *Gilbert v. California*,[2] *Stovall v. Denno*,[3] *Simmons v. United States*,[4] and *Rigney v. Hendrick*,[5] have all affected the police lineup. These decisions should be studied by officers who are involved in either live lineups or photo lineups. They have made lineups subject to the Sixth Amendment right for counsel to be present during the lineup and have made the police extremely careful in conducting the lineup. Officers must select individuals who are similar to the suspect and must have several persons included in the lineup (usually five to eight). For example, *Simmons v. United States* offered suggestions to officers on how photographs should be used to identify a subject.

Another recent use of videotape is for the recording of role-playing situations. Many police academies and training centers are using role playing as an integral part of the training process. In role playing, trained actors and actresses are used to enact realistic situations in which officers are placed to gauge their actions and reactions.

One common type of role playing is in training officers to respond to domestic disputes. Officers respond to a situation in which husband and wife are having an argument. The actions of

---

[1] United States v. Wade, 388 U.S. 218, 87 S.Ct. 1926, 18 L.Ed.2d 1149 (1967)

[2] Gilbert v. California, 388 U.S. 263, 87 S.Ct., 18 L.Ed.2d 1178 (1967)

[3] Stovall v. Denno, 388 U.S. 293, 87 S.Ct. 1967, 18 L.Ed.2d 1199 (1967)

[4] Simmons v. United States, 390 U.S. 377, 88 S.Ct. 967, 19 L.Ed.2d 1247 (1968)

[5] Rigney v. Hendrick, 355 F.2d 710 (3d Cir. 1965), *cert. denied*, 384 U.S. 975, 86 S.Ct. 1868, 16 L.Ed.2d 685 (1966)

the married couple are realistic and unpredictable, and the recruit must act accordingly. The officers are to react as they would in a real-life situation. It is surprising how the officers react to this training. One officer stated at the completion of the situation, "It was just like I was really in the midst of a domestic fight, the sweat was pouring off of my forehead and my hands were shaking."

When the situation is videotaped, the recruit is able to see just how he reacted in the scene and how his clients reacted to his actions. The instructor and the class are also able to critique the officer's performance and to judge his overall effectiveness in controlling and placating the situation. Videotape coupled with role playing has been found to be an excellent training tool.

The various uses of video equipment that were mentioned in this chapter are present methods of utilizing the equipment. Officers and administrators should attempt to develop others ways to put the equipment into service. They should never be limited to known uses but should search for the unknown.

APPENDICES

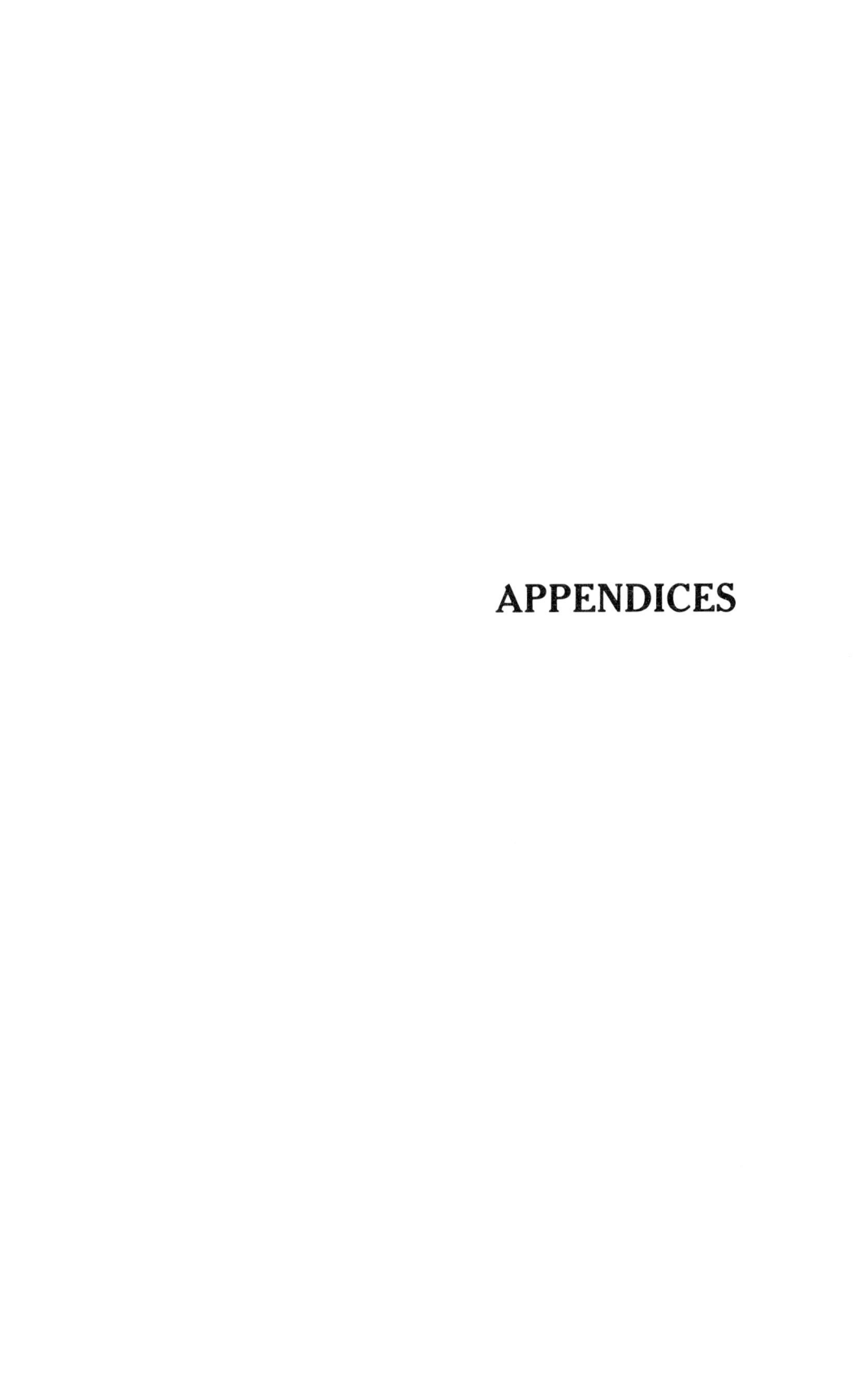

Appendix A

MAJOR MANUFACTURERS

Akai America Ltd.
2139 East Del Amo Blvd.
Compton, CA 90220

Hitachi Sales Corporation
401 Artesia Blvd.
Compton, CA 90220

JVC Industries
50–35 65th Road
Maspeth, NY 11378

Magnavox
1700 Magnavox Way
Fort Wayne, IN 46804

Panasonic Video Systems
One Panasonic Way
Secaucus, NJ 07904

Sony Corporation
9 West 57th Street
New York, NY 10019

Toshiba America
82 Totowa Road
Wayne, NJ 07470

Zenith Corporation
1100 Seymour Street
Franklin Park, IL 60131

Appendix B

TELEVISION RELEASE FORM

Date: _____

I hereby authorize, consent, and give permission to the _____ Police Department to replay, without time restrictions, any recorded appearances and/or performances of myself and my below listed child or ward.

In addition, I authorize, consent and give permission, without time restrictions, to the _____ Police Department to distribute beyond the confines of its own television playback network, any programs that include performances and/or appearances of myself and my below listed child or ward.

NAME _____ AGE _____

Appendix C

PROGRAM SCRIPT

TITLE _____ PAGE _____ OF ___

SHOT	VIDEO	AUDIO

Appendix D

VIDEOTAPE OPERATOR'S STATEMENT FORM

B # _____
Seq. Case # _____

*STATEMENT OF THE CAMERA/VTR OPERATOR
AT THE BEGINNING OF THE TAPE*

I AM _____, Badge # _____ OF THE WYCKOFF POLICE DEPARTMENT. TODAY IS _____, 19_____, AND IT IS PRESENTLY _____ a.m./p.m. I WILL BE OPERATING THE CAMERA AND VIDEOTAPE RECORDER DURING THE QUESTIONING OF AND ADMINISTRATION OF COORDINATION TESTS TO _____ RESIDING AT _____, _____.

_____ WAS ARRESTED AT _____ a.m./p.m. ON (Day of Week) _____, _____, 19_____, FOR DRIVING WHILE UNDER THE INFLUENCE OF LIQUOR OR DRUGS (39:4–50).

Videotape Operator's Statement Form

TAPING OF THIS INDIVIDUAL STARTS AT TAPE COUNTER # _____ AND ENDS AT TAPE COUNTER # _____. TAPING BEGAN AT _____ a.m./p.m. AND ENDED AT _____ a.m./p.m. TOTAL TAPING TIME _____.

_____
Taping Officer's Signature

_____   _____
Witness   DATE

Appendix E

ARRESTING OFFICER'S STATEMENT FORM

B # _____
Seq. Case # _____

VIDEOTAPE PROCEDURE
ARRESTING OFFICER

The primary responsibility of the arresting officer is to protect and assist the camera operator.

START READ
Mr. _____, I am _____ of the _____
    Defendant's Name   Rank and Name

Police Department. At _____ on ____, 19_____,
                  time of arrest date

I arrested you for operating a motor vehicle under the influence of an intoxicating liquor or a narcotic or habit-producing drug.

_____ will operate the videotape camera, which will
camera operator

make a record of everything you do or say while the camera is operating.

You and your attorney will be permitted to view the tape before your trial.

_____
Signature of Arresting Officer

Appendix F

CHAIN OF EVIDENCE WAIVER FORM

CASE # _____
TAPE # _____

ON $\underline{\quad\quad}_{\text{DATE}}$ AT $\underline{\quad\quad}_{\text{TIME}}$, $\underline{\quad\quad\quad\quad\quad\quad}_{\text{DEFENSE ATTORNEY}}$ VIEWED A VIDEOTAPE OF $\underline{\quad\quad\quad}_{\text{DEFENDANT}}$, WHO WAS ARRESTED FOR DRIVING UNDER THE INFLUENCE ON $\underline{\quad\quad}_{\text{DATE}}$ BY OFFICER _____.

* * * * * * * *

ON THE ABOVE DATE, I VIEWED A VIDEOTAPE OF $\underline{\quad\quad\quad}_{\text{DEFENDANT}}$. THE TAPE WAS SHOWN BY OFFICER _____ OF THE _____ POLICE DEPARTMENT. I HEREBY STIPULATE TO THE CHAIN OF EVIDENCE CONCERNING THIS VIDEOTAPE.

_____ _____
DATE   SIGNATURE OF DEFENSE ATTORNEY

THE ENVELOPE THAT CONTAINED THE VIDEOTAPE WAS UNSEALED AND RESEALED IN MY PRESENCE.

_____
SIGNATURE OF DEFENSE ATTORNEY

THE ABOVE VIDEOTAPE WAS VIEWED BY SIGNATURE OF DEFENSE ATTORNEY

GLOSSARY

—A—

AGC. Automatic gain control. Electronic circuitry automatically adjusts video and/or audio signals for proper levels.

Aperture. Regulates the amount of light that passes through the lens (f-stop).

Aspect ratio. The proportion of the television screen, i.e., four parts wide by three parts high.

Assemble edit. The technique of electronically adding a new segment to the end of a recorded tape.

Audio. Sound portion of a television or film production.

Audition. A tryout or test, as in a part for a play.

—B—

Back light. A light source coming from a position opposite that of the camera.

Barn doors. Metal flaps fitted to a spot- or floodlight to control light output and direction.

Battery pack. Portable power source for recorder/camera units.

Beta. Greek word for magnetic flux. Also, Sony's brand for ½-inch videocassette system.

B.G. Abbreviation for background.

Boom. (a) To move camera either up or down. (b) A microphone on a long pole that follows actors on stage.

Bulk eraser. A device that emits a strong electromagnetic field capable of erasing recorded tapes.

Burn-in. Black spots or streaks caused by excessive light striking camera pickup tube.

—C—

Cable. (a) Shielded wire for conducting video/audio signals. (b) Means of television transmission, i.e., cable TV.

Camera brace. Device worn over the shoulder that serves as camera support for hand-held use.

Cardioid. A type of microphone pickup pattern distinguished by its heart shape.

CATV. Community antenna television.

CCTV. Closed-circuit television.

Character generator. An electronic device that generates letter forms and graphics suitable for incorporation into a video signal.

Coaxial. A type of transmission cable noted for its ability to reject interference signals by virtue of its heavy shield. RG59/U is one type used for video applications.

Color temperature. The hue or color quality of light—warm (tungsten) to cool (daylight) measured in degrees Kelvin.

Condenser microphone. A microphone noted for its wide range and sensitivity utilizing a battery as a power source.

Contrast. Amount of difference between light and dark in a picture.

Cover shot. Establishing shot.

Crawl. Technique in which titles or credits are slowly scrolled upwards from the bottom of the screen.

Credits. Names of personnel responsible for a production.

CU. Close-up.

Cue. An indication of when a scripted action begins.

Cut. (a) A sudden change in scene caused by editing or camera switching. (b) Signal to stop action.

—D—

Dead. Not live, as in electronic components not activated or working.

Depth of field. Optical concept dealing with the amount of distance in front of and behind the focused object that appears clear.

Dissolve. A special effect in which one picture slowly fades out while another slowly fades in, indicative of passage of time.

Glossary

Dolly. (a) A wheeled device upon which a camera and tripod are mounted, allowing free and easy camera movement. (b) The technique of moving the camera/dolly assembly in or out of the action. Unlike zoom, this technique changes viewer/camera perspective. *Example:* DOLLY IN/DOLLY OUT.

Dropout. Loss of picture quality during playback resulting in black or white streaks or spots.

Dub. (a) To insert new audio and/or video material over an existing recording. (b) To copy a tape from one recorder to another.

Dynamic. A microphone characterized by its ruggedness and wide pickup range.

—E—

ECU. Extreme close-up.

Edit (editing). Technique of arranging various shots in a sequence to give meaning.

EIAJ. Electronic Industries Association of Japan.

Essential area. That portion of the television picture which is not subject to cropping (loss of picture edges) during transmission.

Establishing shot. Usually the opening shot in a production that orients the viewer to the visual situation.

—F—

f-stop. Lens opening (aperture) corresponding to a standard number system, such as f-5.6, which indicates the amount of light the lens will transmit.

Fact sheet (rundown sheet). A list of objects, people, and activities that will appear before the camera.

Fade-in. A special effect in which picture intensity gradually increases until it appears normal. In audio, volume gradually increases to normal.

Fade-out (fade to black). A special effect in which the picture slowly decreases in intensity until it is black. In audio, the volume gradually decreases to zero.

Field. A half-frame of video picture information. Two fields make one frame at the rate of thirty per second.

Fill light. A diffused light source that serves to remove any dark shadows, particularly from actors' faces.

Flagging. A playback problem in which the top portion of the television picture is pulled left or right, resulting in a waving, flaglike effect.

Follow focus. The technique of continuously focusing on a moving object.

Format. (a) The particular system employed by various videorecording devices. (b) The type of script being used.

—H—

HDTV. High definition television.

Head. The electromagnetic device that enables magnetic impulses to be imparted to magnetically sensitized tape, either audio or video.

Helical scan. Slant track recording system used by ¾-inch and ½-inch videorecording units.

—I—

Insert edit. A type of editing in which a new segment of videotape is electronically placed between existing portions of a recorded tape.

—K—

Kelvin. Temperature scale relative to color of light and measured in degrees.

Key light. The primary light source in a studio setup, which reveals basic form and structure.

—L—

Lapel mike. A cardioid microphone clipped to a collar or lapel.

Lavalier mike. A cardioid microphone that is hung by a strap around the neck.

Lens. The image-forming optical system.

—M—

Med. shot. Approximates a view that shows two people from waist to head.

Mike. Abbreviation for microphone (also **Mic**).

Monopod. A one-legged tripod, used for camera support.

—N—

Newvicon. A television pickup tube known for its light sensitivity and resistance to smear.

—O—

Omnidirectional. A microphone pickup pattern that is sound sensitive from all directions.

Open reel. A recording format that uses open reels of tape rather than cassettes, similar to reel-to-reel audio recorders.

—P—

Pan. A camera technique in which the camera is swiveled left and/or right.

Preview. (a) An advance showing of a production. (b) A control room monitor that allows the director to see the shot before it is put on the air or into recording.

—R—

Recorder. A device that preserves magnetic impulses from video and/or audio signals.

Rehearse. A practice run of a performance.

RF converter. An electronic device that converts video and audio signals into radio frequencies, which can be transmitted through a wire and into the antenna terminals of a television receiver, where it can be reconstituted into a normal TV picture and sound.

Running time. The play time of a production.

—S—

Saticon. A very light-sensitive television pickup tube.

Scanning area. The total picture area of a television frame.

Script. An outline or plan, usually with directions for both sound and picture.

SEG. Abbreviation for special effects generator, an electronic device that allows mixing, switching, and special effects with video.

Slant track. A recording technique (also known as helical scan) in which diagonal bands of information are recorded on a videotape.

Smear. A phenomenon in which bright lights or colors tend to streak and remain visible for a few seconds after a camera is panned, or moved, to a new shot.

Sound. Same as audio.

Stand by. To be in a state of readiness prior to a taping or before going on the air.

Storyboard. A picture outline of a planned production.

Stretch. To extend or expand a time segment, to fill in.

Superimpose. To place one picture over another simultaneously, such as a double exposure.

—T—

Tape. A strip of plasticlike material of varying lengths and widths with a magnetic oxide coating, used for recording video and audio signals.

Telephoto. A lens that magnifies images to make them appear closer.

Tilt. To aim the camera up or down.

Track. A camera technique in which a camera follows action by moving along with it.

Tripod. A three-legged device that is used as a camera support.

—U—

UHF. Ultra high frequency bands for transmission of television signals.

Unidirectional. A microphone pickup pattern that is sound sensitive in one direction.

—V—

VHF. Very high frequency bands for transmission of television signals.

VHS. Video Home System. One half-inch videocassette system.

Video. The picture portion of a television signal.

Vidicon. A television pickup tube of moderate light sensitivity.

VU meter. A volume unit meter, which measures audio levels.

—Z—

Zoom. An effect produced by using a special (zoom) lens, which allows the focal length to change continuously and smoothly, giving the illusion of moving closer or farther away from the subject.

BIBLIOGRAPHY

Books

1. *Independent Video,* Ken Marsh, Straight Arrow Books, 1974, 65 Third Street, San Francisco, CA 94107.
2. *Introducing the Single-Camera VTR System,* Grason Mattingly and Welby Smith, Charles Scribner's Sons, New York, 1973.
3. *The Technique of the Television Cameraman,* Peter Jones, Communication Arts Books, Hastings House Publishers, Inc., 1972, 10 East 40th Street, New York, NY 10016.
4. *The Technique of Television Production,* Gerald Millerson, Communication Arts Books, Hastings House Publishers, Inc., 1975, 10 East 40th Street, New York, NY 10016.
5. *Television Production Handbook,* Herbert Zettle, 2nd ed., Wadsworth Publishing Co., Belmont, CA, 1968.
6. *The Video Handbook,* Media Horizons, Inc., 750 Third Ave., New York, NY.
7. *Video Support in the Criminal Courts,* United States Department of Justice, Law Enforcement Assistance Administration, Washington, D.C., October 1975.
8. *Video Tape Recording,* Charles Bensinger, Petersen Publishing Co., 8490 Sunset Blvd., Los Angeles, CA, 1973.

Periodicals

1. *Photomethods,* P.O. Box 671, Neptune, NJ 07753; $10.00 per year.
2. *Videography,* United Business Publications, 750 Third Avenue, New York, N.Y. 10017; $10.00 per year.

INDEX

A

Adaptor, audio, 45, fig. 16
AGC, 22, 68
Assemble edit, *see* Editing
Assessment of needs, 9-12
Audio, 63-69

B

Batteries, 24, 25, 52, fig. 20
Beta, *see* Videorecorder
Broadcast TV, 5, 6
Bulk eraser, 43, 113

C

CATV, 6
C-mount, 37, 119, 120
Camera operator, *see* Operator
Camera switcher, 50
Cameras, video, 31-39, fig.10,11,12,13,14
    care of, 39
    Newvicon, 32
    Plumbicon, 31
    Saticon, 31
    techniques, 37
    Vidicon, 31
    viewfinders, electronic and optical, 33
CCTV, 7, 37, 138-141
    cameras, 138
    multi-camera, 139
    time-lapse recorder, 139
    uses of, 138-141
Certification of operator
    certificates, 95, 101
    student certified list, 96
Closed circuit television, *see* CCTV

Confessions, 135-137
Court security, 146
Crawl, 54, 126, fig.21
Crime scenes, 132-134
CVC, *see* Videorecorder

D

DBS, 8
Demonstrations or riots, 146
Departmental training, 123-127
    actors, 125
    make up, 125
    props, 125
    roll call training, 123
    selecting subject material, 126
    subject development, 124,125
    tapes, production of, 123-127
    titles, 126
Depositions, 145
Depth of field, 36, 37
Discovery, 111, 112
Dolly, 49
Domestic disputes, 147
Drunk driving
    audio/video check, 107
    auxiliary lighting, 105,107
    checklist, 92
    clock and calendar, 104,105, 108, fig.26
    coordination test taping, 107
    courtroom presentation, 113
    discovery, 111, 112
    equipment set up and operation, 92, 93,
        97-115, fig. 27, 28, 29, 30, 31
    erasing tapes, 112
    hands on instruction, 93
    judicial assistance, 99
    log book, 103, 110

Drunk driving (*Continued*)
   microphones, 105
   mock courtroom, 94
   officer's checklist, 105, 107–109
   problems of, 97, 98
   program, implementation of, 99–114
   room selection for taping, 103
   statistics, 97, 98
   storage of drunk driving tapes, 111, 112
   tape counter setting, 107
   test tape, 107

E

Editing, 70, 76
   assemble edit, 22, 72–74, fig.24
   convergence editing, 76
   insert edit, 22, 72, 75
EIAJ, 17
ENG, 16
Essential area, 34

F

Formats, equipment, *see* Videorecorder
Formats, program, 81, 82

H

HDTV, 8

I

Insert edit, *see* Editing
Instructor, video, 90–96

J

Jack, video, 47, fig.17
Jacks, audio, 45, 47, fig.16
Judicial approval, 90

K

Kinescope, 14

L

Lenses

   care of, 39
   fixed focal length, 35
   telephoto, 35
   tele extender, 119, 120
   wide angle, 35
   zoom, 35
Lesson plans, 90, 91
   lesson objective, 11, 90
   performance objective, 11, 90
Lighting, 57–62
   accessories, 62
   auxiliary for DD, 105, 107
   back light, 61, fig.22
   direct, 57
   direction, 58
   fill light, 60, fig.22
   indirect, 57, 58
   intensity, 59
   key light, 60, fig. 22
   quality, 57, 58
   temperature, 58, 59
Line ups, 147

M

Methods of Instruction, *see* MOI
Microphone, 63–69
   mixer, 50, fig.18
   pick up patterns, 64, 65, fig.23
   special uses, 105, 118
   types, 65, 118
Mixer, microphone, 50, fig.18
Modulator, 53, 54
MOI, 91, 92
Monitor, 20, 21, 52

N

Needs, assessing, 9–12
Newvicon, 32
Nonbroadcast TV, 5, 7

O

Objective, performance, 11, 91
Operator, video
   in courts, 89
   in DD taping, 105, 107, 108, 111–113
   training, 89–96

Index

P

Performance objective, 11, 91
Plugs, audio, 45, 47, fig.16
Plugs, video, 47, fig.17
Plumbicon, 31
Public relations, 142–144
    cable tv in, 143
    model release, 144
    music, 144

Q

Quad (quadruplex), *see* Videorecorder

R

Recruit training, 148
RF, 19–21, 24, 47
Role playing, 147

S

Saticon, 31
Scanning area, 34
Scripting, 81, 85, 125
Search warrants, 146
SEG, 51, 52, fig.19
Signal splitter, 53
Special effects generator, *see* SEG
Stopwatch, 47
Surveillance, 116–122
    body transmitters, 118
    C-mount lens, 119, 120
    car power adaptor, 120
    lenses, 119–120
    microphones, 118
    special camera tubes, 118
    tele extender, 119
    television screen, photographing from, 121, 122
    uses of film, 116, 117
    uses of video tape, 117, 122
Switcher, camera, 50
Super 8 video, 25

T

Tele extender, 119

Television
    broadcast, 5, 6
    CATV, 6
    CCTV, 7, 37
    DBS, 8
    HDTV, 8
    nonbroadcast TV, 5, 7
Television screen, photographing from, 121, 122
Time lapse recorder, 22, 139
Titling, 78–80, 126
Traffic, 128–131
    counts, 128
    educating the public, 130
    evaluation of, 128
    flow studies, 129
    motor vehicle accidents, 129
    surveys, 128
    training, 130
tripod, 37, 49

V

VCR, *see* Videorecorder
VHS, *see* Videorecorder
VHS–C, *see* Videorecorder
Video operator, *see* operator
Videorecorder
    advantages of VCR vs. open reel, 25–27
    Beta, 12, 15, 17, 41, 42, fig.6,9
    CVC, 13
    EIAJ, 22, 139
    maintenance, 28–30, 113, 114
    open reel format, 13, 15, 17, 18, fig.3,4,5,25
    quad (quadruplex), 13, 15
    ¾-inch videocassette, 13, 25, 27, 41, 42, fig.2
    time lapse, 22, 139
    VCR, *see* 3/4-inch cassette, Beta, VHS
    VHS, 13, 25, 27, 41, 42, fig.1,7
    VHS–C, 13, 25, fig.8
Video tape, 40–44
    Beta, 42, fig.15
    inventory, 43
    open reel, 41, fig.15
    other uses of, 145–148
    storage of, 43, 44, 111, 112
    ¾″ videocassette, fig.15

Video tape (*Continued*)
    VHS, 41, 42, fig.15
Vidicon, 31
Viewfinder, optical and electronic, 33

Z

Zoom lens, *see* Lenses